CONTENTS

Chapter 1

THE MAGIC OF INDUCTION COOKING

THERE ARE SO MANY REASONS TO DISCOVER INDUCTION COOKING! Whether you've acquired a burner to supply an extra cooking surface in your kitchen, plan to take it on the road for your next camping trip, or cook in a space that otherwise wouldn't have a cooktop, you can rely on an induction burner to be a fast, safe, and relatively easy appliance to use. To help you make the most of a powerful tool, this cookbook features dozens of classic, family-favorite recipes created to maximize the potential induction cooking can offer. So, let's get started!

HOW DOES IT WORK?

At first glance, you might think that your induction burner, with its smooth glassy surface, looks a lot like a radiant electric cooktop, but there are some important differences. An electric cooktop radiates heat by passing electricity through a heating element that turns warm and will heat up anything that touches it. Your induction burner, on the other hand, contains tightly wound copper coils beneath its surface, and when electric current runs through them, it produces a magnetic field. This field "induces" heat in ferrous cookware (any cookware that contains iron, including most steel). Because induction cooking uses electromagnetism to heat pots and pans, it accomplishes the task significantly faster. But speed is just one of the benefits.

the magnet test

Use a magnet to see whether your cookware will work on an induction cooktop. If it contains a ferrous metal, a magnet sticks to the side of your pan with a strong hold. However, keep in mind that because induction relies on a direct contact with the cooking surface, any slight warps in the bottom of the pan could affect performance.

REAL (DELICIOUS!) BENEFITS

Think of your induction cooktop as one tool that can perform many tricks. On its lowest settings you can use it as a double boiler for making fondue or melting chocolate. Look to the recipes for Favorite Cheese Fondue (page 112) or Peanut Butter–Chocolate Fondue (page 126) to see how it works. Alternatively, when you use a cast-iron Dutch oven with your induction cooktop, you have all you need to harness the power of slow cooking—with one important difference. If you begin with a higher heat setting, you can lock in the flavor of your meats with a quick sear and then turn the heat down to create a slow cooking environment. The best part of that scenario: you only use one pot! Check out the recipes for Slow-Cooked Beef Stew (page 62) and Home-Style Chicken & Dumplings (page 85) to see for yourself how easy it can be.

Yet another benefit: induction cooking is ideally suited for warmer weather when the last thing you want to do is heat up your kitchen. Consider how a gas flame, for example, releases lots of heat around the pan, and an electric burner emits radiant heat at any point where it's not in direct, firm contact with the pan. When heat is generated within the pan itself, as with induction, more of that heat gets to the food, and less of it warms up your kitchen. The difference is noticeable.

And for that same reason, induction cooking is quite a bit safer than many other cooking methods. While all cooking methods require careful attention in the kitchen, the efficiency of induction cooking means that your pan's response to a turn of the dial is practically immediate. So as soon as you turn off the heat, the pan cools down. And once you remove your cookware from the cooktop, the cooktop starts to cool down, too.

INDUCTION COOKING TIPS

Because induction cooking is fast and efficient, pay extra close attention to your dish as it cooks. Induction cooktops vary slightly from model to model. Most include numbered settings that correspond to specific temperatures. For that reason, the instructions within this collection are written to indicate a temperature setting, but you should adapt the recipes as you see fit to match the settings on your model as closely as possible. Consult your owner's manual to see how the ranges in our chart compare to the settings on your induction cooktop, and as always use your best judgment in the kitchen.

TEMPERATURE	LEVEL
100°F–110°F	WARM
150°F	LOW
180°F–210°F	MEDIUM-LOW
240°F–270°F	MEDIUM
300°F–360°F	MEDIUM–HIGH
390°F–450°F	HIGH

Now, get ready to love your induction burner—and the amazing recipes it will cook with ease, efficiency, and flavor! You'll wonder why you waited to try induction cooking.

Chapter 2

BREAKFASTS +BRUNCHES

Maple-Pear
OATMEAL

OATMEAL IS A QUICK AND EASY BREAKFAST option that is often overlooked because so many recipes out there are basic and bland. This outrageously good oatmeal is not one of those recipes! Taste what a difference the right combination of ingredients precisely cooked on your induction burner can make. Not crazy about pears? Simply substitute bananas.

2 cups water

1 cup rolled oats

⅓ cup walnuts, coarsely chopped

1 tablespoon unsalted butter

1 large pear, peeled, cored, and sliced

3 tablespoons maple syrup

Dash of ground cinnamon or allspice

Pinch of salt

2 tablespoons heavy cream (optional)

In a medium ferrous-bottomed saucepan, bring the water to a boil over high heat (390°F). Stir in the oats and reduce the heat to medium-low (180°F). Cook for 3 to 5 minutes, stirring occasionally, until the oats are thickened. Set the pan on a heatproof surface while you prepare the pecans and pears.

In a small ferrous-bottomed nonstick skillet, toast the walnuts over medium heat (270°F), stirring occasionally, until the nuts are beginning to brown and become fragrant. Tip the nuts onto a plate to cool.

In the same skillet, warm the butter over medium heat (270°F). When the butter has melted, add the pear and cook until softened, 3 to 4 minutes. Turn off the cooktop and add the syrup, cinnamon or allspice, and salt, and stir until thoroughly combined.

Divide the oatmeal between 2 bowls and top with the pear-syrup mixture and toasted nuts. Drizzle with the cream (if using).

Florentine OMELET

SERVES
1

YOU CAN EASILY WHIP UP YOUR OWN OMELET combinations that rival pricy weekend brunches out—in the privacy of your own kitchen! This method is a classic for making an omelet that yields perfect results. Just remember that to avoid scratching the glass surface of your induction cooktop, always remove the pan before shaking it.

In a ferrous-bottomed nonstick skillet, warm the butter over medium heat (270°F). When the butter has melted, add the onion and cook until translucent, 1 to 2 minutes. Add the spinach and cook, stirring occasionally, until wilted, about 1 minute longer. Pour the eggs into the skillet, remove from the cooktop briefly, and tilt so that the eggs spread evenly over the vegetables; gently shake the skillet a few times so that the eggs coat the bottom of the skillet.

Return the skillet to the cooktop and cook until the eggs are firm but not dry, about 2 minutes longer. Scatter the feta over the top and fold the omelet if desired. Remove the omelet from the skillet; set aside and keep warm. Add the tomatoes to the skillet, cooking for 1 to 2 minutes. Serve the omelet topped with the tomatoes. Season to taste with salt and pepper.

1 tablespoon unsalted butter

2 tablespoons finely chopped onion

1 cup baby spinach

2 eggs, lightly beaten

2 tablespoons crumbled feta

3–4 cherry tomatoes, halved

Salt and freshly ground black pepper

One-Skillet
SHAKSHUKA

SERVES
4

WAKE UP YOUR BREAKFAST WITH A BRIGHT, SPICY start from Middle Eastern cuisine! Because it's packed with satisfying vegetables, shakshuka is also a great option for brunch or a light dinner. And it all comes together in one pan on your induction burner, so cleanup is easy. Serve with pan-grilled bread or whole wheat pitas.

2 tablespoons olive oil

1 small onion, chopped

1 red bell pepper, cored, seeded, and chopped

3 cloves garlic, sliced

2 tablespoons sweet paprika

1 teaspoon ground cumin

1 teaspoon ground coriander

¼ teaspoon kosher salt

1 can (28 ounces) crushed tomatoes

2 teaspoons sugar

8 eggs

2 tablespoons chopped fresh parsley

In a large, ferrous-bottomed nonstick skillet, warm the olive oil over medium heat (270°F). Add the onion, bell pepper, garlic, paprika, cumin, coriander, and salt. Cook for 8 to 10 minutes, stirring occasionally, until the vegetables are softened.

Stir in the tomatoes and sugar. Cook, stirring occasionally, for another 10 minutes until the tomatoes are thickened. Use the back of a spoon to make 8 slight indentations in the sauce.

Working one at a time, crack the eggs into a small bowl and then slide them into the skillet. Reduce the heat to medium-low (180°F). Cover and cook for another 5 minutes, until the eggs are set (10 minutes if you prefer a firm yolk). Garnish with the parsley.

Best-Ever
SCRAMBLED EGGS

SERVES 2

FOR SCRAMBLED EGGS THAT ARE CREAMY and delicious, turn to an induction cooktop! The secret to sensational scrambled eggs is cooking them slowly, which an induction cooktop is ideally suited to do. This recipe is easily doubled if you want to feed and please even more breakfast companions.

4 large eggs, lightly beaten

1 tablespoon cold water

Pinch of salt

2 tablespoons unsalted butter

In a small bowl, beat the eggs with the water and salt. Set aside.

In small ferrous-bottomed nonstick skillet over medium-low heat (180°F), melt the butter. When the butter begins to foam, add the eggs and cook without stirring until the mixture begins to set on the bottom and edges. Use a silicone spatula or wooden spoon to gently push the egg curds into the center of the skillet so that the uncooked liquid flows to the empty parts of the skillet. Continue cooking, moving the eggs gently to ensure even cooking, to desired doneness, 2 to 3 minutes longer.

Raisin-Bread
FRENCH TOAST
with Vanilla Sauce

SERVES
4

TAKE TRADITIONAL FRENCH TOAST TO A NEW LEVEL—without adding tons of ingredients or extra work! Simply swapping in raisin bread adds a delicious twist. The bread pairs perfectly with the vanilla sauce, which is a bit lighter than maple syrup and comes together so easily with the help of your precise induction cooktop.

TO MAKE THE FRENCH TOAST: In a large shallow bowl, whisk together the eggs and milk. Soak the bread in the egg mixture, turning to coat.

Melt 1 tablespoon of the butter in a large, ferrous-bottomed nonstick skillet over medium-high heat (360°F). Arrange 4 slices of bread in the skillet and cook until browned, 2 to 4 minutes. Flip the bread and cook on the other side until lightly browned. Transfer the toast to a plate and cover to keep warm. Melt the remaining 1 tablespoon of butter and repeat with the remaining 4 slices of bread.

TO MAKE THE VANILLA SAUCE: Reduce the heat to medium (240°F). Melt the 2 tablespoons butter in the skillet and add the brown sugar. Stir until the sugar melts and begins to bubble. Add the vanilla extract and salt.

Serve the French toast topped with the vanilla sauce.

FRENCH TOAST

3 eggs, lightly beaten

1 cup milk

8 slices raisin bread

2 tablespoons unsalted butter, divided

VANILLA SAUCE

2 tablespoons unsalted butter

½ cup brown sugar

1 teaspoon vanilla extract

Pinch of salt

Blueberry-
BUTTERMILK
PANCAKES

SERVES
4

PUT A STACK OF THESE BEAUTIES ON THE TABLE, and everyone will gather around to enjoy! While blueberries are admittedly a fresh summertime favorite, you can easily use frozen berries in this recipe—keep a bag on hand. A round cast-iron griddle is the perfect surface for cooking pancakes on an induction burner, but a skillet works, too.

In a large bowl, stir together the flour, sugar, baking powder, baking soda, and salt. Whisk in the buttermilk, eggs, and melted butter, just until combined. Stir in the blueberries.

Heat a small knob of butter in a large ferrous-bottomed nonstick skillet or griddle over medium-high heat (360°F). When a few drops of water sizzle on the skillet, ladle ⅓ cup of batter at a time to make the pancakes. Flip the pancakes when bubbles rise to the surface and the bottoms brown, 2 to 4 minutes.

Cook until the second side is lightly browned. Transfer the pancakes to a plate and repeat until all the batter is used. Serve with maple syrup.

2 cups all-purpose flour

1 tablespoon sugar

2 teaspoons baking powder

1 teaspoon baking soda

1 teaspoon salt

2½ cups buttermilk

2 large eggs, lightly beaten

¼ cup unsalted butter, melted, plus additional butter for griddle

2 cups blueberries (fresh or frozen)

Maple syrup, for serving

Creamy
SAUSAGE GRAVY

TRADITIONALLY SERVED WITH BUTTERMILK BISCUITS, sausage gravy is a flavor-packed topping that works just as nicely over toast (if you've no time to bake biscuits) or breakfast potatoes. It's so simple to whip up on your induction cooktop!

1 pound breakfast sausage

½ cup all-purpose flour

3 cups milk, preferably whole or 2%

Salt and freshly ground black pepper

Tear the sausage into small pieces and arrange in a large, ferrous-bottomed nonstick skillet. Cook over medium-high heat (330°F), stirring occasionally, until lightly browned, 10 to 15 minutes.

Sprinkle the flour over the sausage and continue cooking until the flour is completely absorbed, about 5 minutes. Stirring constantly, slowly pour in the milk. Continue cooking, stirring occasionally, until the gravy reaches the desired thickness (add a little more milk if it becomes too thick). Season to taste with salt and pepper.

Anytime
POTATO PANCAKES

SERVES
4

THESE PANCAKES MAKE A SATISFYING BREAKFAST, although they are also delicious served as an appetizer topped with a small piece of smoked salmon and a dollop of sour cream. So many ways to enjoy, just like your induction burner!

Using a food processor fitted with a coarse grating blade, shred the potatoes and onion. Transfer the vegetables to a colander placed over a large bowl and toss with the salt. Let them sit for 15 minutes to drain. Squeeze as much liquid as you can from the potato mixture (collecting the liquid that accumulates) and transfer the vegetables to another large bowl. Let the liquid sit for a few minutes to settle, then pour the liquid from the bowl, reserving the starch that has settled in the bottom of the bowl. Add the reserved potato starch, eggs, flour, and baking powder to the potato mixture and stir until thoroughly combined. Season to taste with pepper.

In a large, deep ferrous-bottomed skillet over medium–high heat (340°F), heat ½ inch of oil. When the oil is hot, use 2 spoons to slide heaping tablespoons of the pancake mixture into the hot oil and fry, turning once, until golden brown, 3 to 4 minutes per side. Drain on paper towels and serve warm with applesauce and sour cream on the side.

1½ pounds Idaho potatoes, peeled

1 small onion, peeled

1½ teaspoons salt

2 eggs, lightly beaten

2 tablespoons all-purpose flour

¼ teaspoon baking powder

Freshly ground black pepper

Vegetable oil, for frying

1 cup applesauce

½ cup sour cream

Classic
MONTE CRISTO SANDWICH

SLICED HAM AND MELTED CHEDDAR CHEESE on bread perfectly browned on your induction cooktop . . . hungry yet? These "knife-and-fork" sandwiches are a variation on French toast with the savory additions that make them work beyond everyday breakfast for a weekend brunch or comforting weeknight supper.

4 slices sandwich bread

2 tablespoons cherry preserves

¼ pound thinly sliced ham

4 slices Cheddar cheese

2 eggs, lightly beaten

½ cup milk

2 tablespoons unsalted butter

1 tablespoon confectioners' sugar

Spread 2 slices of bread with the cherry preserves and top with the ham and cheese. Cover with the remaining slices of bread. In a large shallow bowl, whisk together the eggs and milk.

Melt the butter in a large, ferrous-bottomed nonstick skillet over medium heat (240°F). Dip the sandwiches in the egg mixture and carefully add to the skillet. Cook until browned, 3 to 4 minutes. Flip and cook until browned on the other side, 3 to 4 minutes. Sprinkle with the confectioners' sugar just before serving.

Hearty
BEEF HASH

YOUR DINNER LEFTOVERS CAN TASTE DELICIOUS the next morning when you transform them into a hearty breakfast hash. Feel free to substitute roast turkey or pork for the beef—the flavors will meld just as nicely with the key ingredients when heated on the induction cooktop.

¼ cup unsalted butter, divided

1 small onion, finely chopped

3 cooked russet potatoes, chopped

1 pound cooked pot roast, chopped (about 3 cups)

1 teaspoon Worcestershire sauce

1 tablespoon chopped fresh parsley

Salt and freshly ground black pepper

8 eggs

Hot sauce (optional)

Melt 2 tablespoons of the butter in a large, ferrous-bottomed nonstick skillet over medium heat (240°F). Add the potatoes and cook the onion until lightly browned, 10 to 15 minutes. Add the beef, Worcestershire sauce, and parsley, and continue cooking, stirring occasionally, until the beef is warmed through. Season to taste with salt and pepper. Transfer the mixture to serving bowls and set aside.

Melt the remaining 2 tablespoons of butter in the same skillet over medium heat (240°F). Add the eggs and cook until the tops of the whites are set but the yolks are still runny, 3 to 4 minutes.* Serve the eggs over the hash mixture. Top with a splash of hot sauce (if using).

Young children, the elderly, and pregnant women may have weaker immune systems, which can put them at a higher risk of contracting foodborne illnesses, such as salmonella. To be on the safe side, make sure that the yolks on their fried eggs are fully cooked, not runny as suggested above.

Boston BROWN BREAD

LOAVES
2

UNLIKE MOST BREADS, BROWN BREAD IS STEAMED rather than baked, making it ideal for your induction cooktop. Traditionally, this bread is made with a 1-pound coffee can and a tall pot with a rack inside to hold it, but you can also use two empty 28-ounce cans, as directed here.

Grease and flour 2 empty 28-ounce cans. Set aside.

In a large bowl, combine the flours, cornmeal, baking soda, salt, and raisins. Make a well in the center and add the buttermilk and molasses. Stir just until moistened.

Transfer the batter to the prepared cans and cover with aluminum foil, ensuring the edges are tightly closed but leaving the foil in the center of the cans a bit loose so the bread can expand. Set the cans on a rack inside a tall, ferrous-bottomed pot. Pour boiling water into the pot until it reaches halfway up the sides of the cans. Cover the pot and place over medium-low heat (180°F) so that the water stays at a simmer. Steam the bread for 2 hours, adding more water to the pot if necessary.

The bread is done when a skewer inserted into the center of the loaf comes out clean. Uncover and allow to cool in the pot for 20 minutes before handling. If necessary, run a knife along the inner edge of the can to unmold. Serve warm or cooled.

½ cup rye flour

½ cup all-purpose flour

½ cup yellow cornmeal

1 teaspoon baking soda

½ teaspoon salt

1 cup raisins

1 cup buttermilk

⅓ cup molasses

Chapter 3

SANDWICHES, SOUPS + SALADS

Golden
GRILLED CHEESE

FORGET ABOUT THOSE OLD-FASHIONED GRILLED CHEESE sandwiches your mother used to make! These decadent sandwiches are crusted in a golden layer of crispy cheese, a feat made all the easier with the precision heating only an induction burner can provide.

2 tablespoons mayonnaise

2 tablespoons grated Parmesan cheese

4 slices sandwich bread

½ cup shredded Cheddar cheese

Combine the mayonnaise and Parmesan in a small bowl. Spread the mixture evenly over the bread slices.

Heat a large, ferrous-bottomed nonstick skillet over medium heat (240°F). Arrange 2 bread slices, mayonnaise-side down, in the skillet and top with the Cheddar. Cover with the remaining bread slices, arranged mayonnaise-side up. Cook until browned, 3 to 4 minutes. Flip and cook until browned on the other side, 3 to 4 minutes.

Grilled
TURKEY SANDWICH
with Brie & Pear

YOU CAN MAKE PRESSED SANDWICHES without one of those fancy griddles. Your induction cooktop maintains a nice low temperature to ensure your sandwich achieves the right combination of well-melted cheese and perfectly toasted bread. Just pair it with a small cast-iron grill press to help flatten your sandwich—you'll save money and storage space.

2 teaspoons Dijon mustard

1 teaspoon honey

4 slices multigrain bread

½ pear, peeled, cored, and sliced

¼ pound sliced turkey

2 ounces Brie cheese, sliced

2 tablespoons unsalted butter

Combine the mustard and honey in a small bowl. Spread the mixture evenly over 2 bread slices and top with the pear, turkey, and Brie. Cover with the remaining bread slices.

Melt the butter in a large, ferrous-bottomed nonstick skillet over medium heat (240°F). Arrange the sandwiches in the skillet and set a grill press on top. Cook until browned, 3 to 4 minutes. Flip and cook until browned on the other side, 3 to 4 minutes.

California
VEGETABLE PANINI
with Bacon

IF YOU LOVE SPINACH-ARTICHOKE DIP, you'll love this vegetable-packed sandwich! The recipe works well with Roma tomatoes, but if garden-fresh tomatoes are available, definitely take advantage and use them. For best results, always begin cooking bacon in a cold skillet; don't preheat it. You'll be amazed by how much more crispy your bacon gets!

Arrange the bacon in a large, ferrous-bottomed nonstick skillet over medium-low heat (210°F). Cook, turning occasionally, until the bacon reaches the desired doneness, 10 to 15 minutes. Transfer the bacon to a plate lined with paper towels and drain any accumulated fats.

Add the spinach and onion to the same skillet, increase the heat to medium (240°F), and cook until the spinach is wilted, 1 to 2 minutes. Remove from the heat and add the artichoke hearts to warm them briefly.

Transfer the vegetables to a medium bowl and add the cream cheese. Use a fork to mash the filling until it is thoroughly combined. Wipe out the skillet.

Spread the filling mixture evenly over 2 slices of bread and top with the reserved bacon and the tomato slices, followed by the remaining slices of bread.

Melt the butter in the same skillet over medium heat (240°F). Arrange the sandwiches in the skillet and set a grill press on top. Cook until browned, 3 to 4 minutes. Flip and cook until browned on the other side, 3 to 4 minutes.

4 slices bacon

1 cup baby spinach

2 tablespoons finely chopped red onion

¼ cup chopped artichoke hearts

¼ cup cream cheese

4 slices sandwich bread

1 Roma tomato, thinly sliced

1 tablespoon unsalted butter

Pressed
CUBAN SANDWICH

SANDWICHES ARE A GREAT WAY TO MAKE THE MOST of a little bit of cooked meat you might have left over. However, these sandwiches are so delicious you might be tempted to start making pork roasts just to have leftovers to work with on your induction cooktop!

Combine the mayonnaise and garlic powder in a small bowl. Spread the mayonnaise mixture evenly over 2 halves of the ciabatta rolls and spread the mustard on the other halves. Arrange half the cheese over half of the rolls, followed by the pork, ham, pickles, and remaining cheese. Set the other half of the ciabatta rolls on top and press the sandwiches lightly to help secure the ingredients.

Melt the butter in the skillet over medium heat (240°F). Arrange the sandwiches in the skillet and set a grill press on top. Cook until browned, 3 to 4 minutes. Flip and cook until browned on the other side, 3 to 4 minutes.

2 tablespoons mayonnaise

½ teaspoon garlic powder

2 ciabatta rolls, split

2 teaspoons yellow mustard

4 slices Swiss cheese

4 ounces cooked pork roast, sliced

2 slices deli ham

8 slices dill pickle

2 tablespoons unsalted butter

Steak & Cheddar
PANINI

SERVES
2

SLICED STEAK WITH CREAMY HORSERADISH: it's a flavor pairing that never loses its appeal! For best results, season the steak and let it rest on the counter for about 30 minutes before cooking (until it is at room temperature). Have leftover steak on hand? Simply slice it and warm it up for a few minutes in the skillet before assembling the sandwiches.

1 (8-ounce) sirloin steak

Salt and freshly ground black pepper

2 tablespoons mayonnaise

1 tablespoon prepared horseradish

2 ciabatta rolls, split

½ cup shredded Cheddar cheese

2 tablespoons unsalted butter

Season the steak generously with salt and pepper. In a large, ferrous-bottomed nonstick skillet over medium-high heat (360°F), cook the steak, flipping halfway through the cooking time, to the desired doneness, 7 to 10 minutes for medium-rare or 9 to 12 minutes for medium. Transfer the steak to a plate and let it rest for 10 minutes before slicing. Wipe out the skillet.

Combine the mayonnaise and horseradish in a small bowl. Spread the mixture evenly over the insides of the ciabatta rolls and fill with the steak and Cheddar. Press the sandwiches lightly to help secure the ingredients.

Melt the butter in the skillet over medium heat (240°F). Arrange the sandwiches in the skillet and set a grill press on top. Cook until browned, 3 to 4 minutes. Flip and cook until browned on the other side, 3 to 4 minutes.

GOAT CHEESE &
CHICKEN QUESADILLAS
with Corn Salsa

**SERVES
4**

YOU CAN FILL A PRESSED TORTILLA with just about anything you like and call it a quesadilla. But creamy goat cheese and grilled chicken are heaven in a tortilla! Although flour tortillas work best for quesadillas, you can still enjoy rich corn flavor with a spoonful of fresh corn salsa on top. It's an especially good option if you're not a fan of tomato-based salsas.

TO MAKE THE SALSA: In a bowl, whisk together the olive oil, lime juice, honey, and cumin. Add the corn, jalapeño, onion, and cilantro. Toss until thoroughly combined. Season to taste with salt and pepper. Set aside while you prepare the quesadillas.

TO MAKE THE QUESADILLAS: Arrange 4 tortillas on a clean work surface and top evenly with the goat cheese and chicken breast slices. Top with the remaining tortillas and press lightly to seal.

Working in batches, heat 1½ teaspoons of the oil in a large, ferrous-bottomed nonstick skillet over medium-high heat (360°F). Gently slide one of the quesadillas into the skillet and cook until lightly browned, 2 to 3 minutes. Carefully flip the quesadilla and continue cooking on the other side until golden, about 2 minutes longer. Repeat with remaining oil and quesadillas. Cut into wedges and serve with the salsa and a dollop of sour cream (if using).

SALSA

1 tablespoon olive oil

1 tablespoon fresh lime juice

1 teaspoon honey

¼ teaspoon ground cumin

1 cup frozen corn, thawed

1 small jalapeño, finely chopped

2 tablespoons finely chopped red onion

2 tablespoons chopped fresh cilantro

Salt and freshly ground black pepper

QUESADILLAS

8 flour tortillas

5 ounces goat cheese, crumbled

1 large grilled chicken breast, thinly sliced

2 tablespoons olive oil, divided

¼ cup sour cream (optional)

Turkey
SLOPPY JOES

GET READY TO TASTE THE BEST SLOPPY JOES you've ever made! The longer the meat simmers, the more flavorful these sandwiches become—and simmering is super easy with the control an induction burner gives you. A hint of pickle relish in this version also adds a nice contrast to the sweetness of the sauce.

1 tablespoon olive oil

1 pound lean ground turkey

1 small onion, chopped

Salt and freshly ground black pepper

½ cup ketchup

2 tablespoons brown sugar

1 tablespoon dill pickle relish

4 hamburger rolls, split

4 slices American cheese (optional)

In a large, ferrous-bottomed nonstick skillet over medium-high heat (360°F), heat the olive oil. Add the turkey and onion. Cook, breaking up the meat with the side of a spoon as it cooks, for 5 minutes, until the turkey is beginning to brown and the onions are softened. Season to taste with salt and pepper.

While the meat is cooking, whisk together the ketchup, sugar, and pickle relish. Reduce the heat to medium-low (180°F). Pour the ketchup mixture over the turkey and stir until evenly coated. Cover and simmer for 20 minutes, stirring occasionally. If you prefer a thicker mixture, uncover for the last 5 minutes. Serve on rolls with cheese (if using).

Easy
AVGOLEMONO

THIS BRIGHT, LEMONY SOUP IS A CLASSIC in Greek cuisine that you need to try. The recipe begins with a homemade chicken stock, but if you're pressed for time, 2 quarts of store-bought broth and about 2 cups of chopped meat from a rotisserie chicken will substitute nicely. Who doesn't love a recipe that adjusts to your needs?

4 skinless, bone-in chicken thighs (about 1½ pounds)

8 cups cold water

1 small onion, halved

1 carrot, peeled and chopped

2 ribs celery, chopped

1 bay leaf

2 teaspoons salt

1 cup long-grain white rice

2 eggs, at room temperature

Juice of 1 lemon

2 tablespoons chopped fresh parsley

Freshly ground black pepper

In a large ferrous-bottomed soup pot or Dutch oven, combine the chicken, water, onion, carrot, celery, bay leaf, and salt over high heat (450°F). When the soup comes to a boil, reduce the heat to medium-low (180°F) and let simmer for 1 hour, until the meat can be easily removed from the bone. Remove the chicken and vegetables from the stock. When it is cool enough to handle, shred the chicken into bite-sized chunks and discard the vegetables and bones. Strain the stock through a colander lined with paper towels and return it to the pot.

Add the rice and cook over medium-high heat (360°F) for 20 minutes, until the rice is tender. Meanwhile, in a medium bowl, beat the eggs and lemon juice until frothy. Ladle 1 cup of stock into the egg mixture and whisk quickly until thoroughly combined. Repeat with another cup of stock, then pour the mixture into the soup pot. Whisk until thoroughly combined and the soup begins to thicken, 4 to 5 minutes. Taste and add more salt, if desired.

Serve the soup topped with shredded chicken and garnished with the parsley and freshly ground black pepper to taste.

Mushroom-
BARLEY SOUP

A LITTLE TIME NOW PAYS OFF LATER: you'll need about 90 minutes to give this soup plenty of simmering on the induction cooktop. However, it reheats well, making it a perfect soup to prepare on the weekend and enjoy later in the week. If you have a food processor handy, break it out to chop vegetables in seconds.

In a large ferrous-bottomed soup pot or Dutch oven, heat the oil over medium-high heat (300°F). Add the mushrooms, celery, carrots, and onion. Cook, stirring occasionally, until the vegetables soften and most of the cooking liquid has evaporated, about 15 minutes.

Add the broth, barley, and bay leaf. Increase the heat to high (450°F). When the soup comes to a boil, reduce the heat to low (180°F) and simmer, partially covered, until the barley is tender, 40 to 60 minutes. Remove the bay leaf, stir in the parsley and sherry (if using), and season to taste with salt and pepper before serving.

2 tablespoons olive oil

1 pound brown mushrooms, trimmed and finely chopped

2 ribs celery, finely chopped

2 carrots, peeled and finely chopped

1 small onion, finely chopped

8 cups vegetable broth

⅔ cup pearl barley

1 bay leaf

¼ cup chopped fresh parsley

2 tablespoons dry sherry (optional)

Salt and freshly ground black pepper

Traditional
MINESTRONE

SERVES
6

THIS HEARTY, SIMPLE-TO-PREPARE SOUP is a meal in a pot! It's no wonder it's a favorite Italian recipe. For a vegetarian version, simply use vegetable broth in place of chicken broth. Don't have the exact veggies the recipe calls for? Swap in whatever's in your fridge. It's flexible and all delicious simmered on the induction burner.

In a large ferrous-bottomed soup pot or Dutch oven, heat the oil over medium-high heat (300°F). Add the onion, potato, carrots, celery, garlic, and oregano. Cook, stirring occasionally, until the vegetables begin to soften, about 5 minutes.

Raise the temperature to high (450°F) and add the tomatoes and broth. When the soup comes to a boil, add the pasta, kidney beans, and green beans. Reduce the heat to medium-low (180°F) and cook, covered, until the pasta is tender, about 20 minutes. Add the parsley and Parmesan (if using) just before serving.

2 tablespoons olive oil

1 large onion, chopped

1 russet potato, peeled and chopped

2 carrots, peeled and chopped

2 ribs celery, chopped

4 cloves garlic, chopped

1 teaspoon dried oregano

1 can (28 ounces) diced tomatoes

6 cups chicken broth

1 cup elbow pasta

1 can (14 ounces) kidney beans, rinsed and drained

8 ounces frozen green beans

2 tablespoons chopped fresh Italian parsley

¼ cup grated Parmesan (optional)

New England
CLAM CHOWDER

RICH AND HEARTY, THIS SOUP IS THE PERFECT bowl of warmth on a cold evening. And because you have precision control over the heat, making cream-based soups with an induction cooktop is especially quick and easy.

3 slices bacon, chopped

1 small onion, finely chopped

1 rib celery, finely chopped

1 large russet potato, chopped (about 2 cups)

1 can (10 ounces) minced clams, drained (reserve the juice)

¾ cup water

¾ teaspoon salt

1½ cups half-and-half

2 tablespoons unsalted butter

2 tablespoons all-purpose flour

2 tablespoons chopped fresh parsley

Freshly ground black pepper

Oyster crackers (optional)

In a medium ferrous-bottomed soup pot over medium heat (240°F), combine the bacon, onion, and celery. Cook for 10 to 15 minutes, until the bacon is browned and the vegetables are soft. Add the potatoes, reserved clam juice, water, and salt. Cover and cook until the potatoes are fork-tender, about 15 minutes. Add the half-and-half and remove the pot from the cooktop to a heatproof surface.

In a small ferrous-bottomed skillet, melt the butter over medium heat (240°F) and whisk in the flour. Cook, whisking regularly, until the mixture is lightly browned, 2 to 3 minutes. Remove from the heat and place the soup pot back on the cooktop.

Slowly whisk the flour mixture into the soup and cook, stirring occasionally, until warmed through, about 5 minutes (do not bring the soup to a boil). Add the clams and parsley. Season to taste with pepper. Top each serving with oyster crackers (if using).

Italian
SAUSAGE-BEAN SOUP

SERVES
6

YOU HAVE A COMPLETE ONE-DISH MEAL with the addition of fresh escarole at the end of the cooking time! Use sweet or hot Italian sausage in the recipe—whatever your palate prefers. This rustic soup is especially delicious served with grilled bread.

In a large ferrous-bottomed soup pot or Dutch oven over medium-high heat (330°F), cook the sausage, breaking it into small pieces with the side of a wooden spoon as it cooks, until browned, about 10 minutes. Add the onion, celery, garlic, and pepper flakes. Cook, stirring occasionally, until the vegetables soften, about 5 minutes.

Add the chicken broth and beans and bring the soup to a boil. Add the escarole, reduce the heat to medium-low (180°F), and let simmer, covered, for 5 minutes to allow flavors to combine. Serve drizzled with the olive oil and sprinkled with the Parmesan (if using).

½ pound Italian sausage, casing removed

1 small onion, finely chopped

1 rib celery, finely chopped

4 cloves garlic, minced

¼ teaspoon red pepper flakes

6 cups chicken broth

2 cans (14 ounces) cannellini beans, rinsed and drained

½ pound escarole, coarsely chopped

2 tablespoons olive oil

¼ cup grated Parmesan (optional)

Beer-Cheese
POTATO SOUP

SERVES
8

THIS SOUP IS A PROVEN CROWD-PLEASER and is sure to score big points if you serve it on game day. However, cheese-based soups can scorch easily when left unattended. That's why using an induction cooktop, which allows you to keep your soup warm at a very low heat, makes the process super simple.

6 slices thick-cut bacon

2 pounds russet potatoes, peeled and coarsely chopped

1 small onion, chopped

2 cups chicken broth

1½ cups milk

1 cup beer, preferably lager

1 tablespoon Worcestershire sauce

1 teaspoon Dijon mustard

¾ teaspoon salt

3 cups shredded Cheddar cheese, divided

4 small sprigs of fresh thyme

In a ferrous-bottomed skillet over medium heat (240°F) cook the bacon, turning occasionally, until crisp, about 10 minutes. Remove to a paper towel to drain. When the bacon is cool enough to handle, crumble it and set it aside.

In a large ferrous-bottomed soup pot or Dutch oven over high heat (450°F), combine the potatoes, onion, and chicken broth and bring to a boil. Cover, reduce the heat to low (180°F), and cook for 20 to 25 minutes, until the potatoes are very tender. Use an immersion blender to puree the potatoes, or work in batches and puree the potatoes in a standing blender.

Whisk in the milk, beer, Worcestershire sauce, mustard, and salt. Raise the heat to medium (270°F) and cook for another 5 minutes, until warmed through. Add 2 cups of cheese, stirring until melted. Top each serving with the reserved bacon, 2 tablespoons of remaining cheese, and ½ sprig of fresh thyme.

Curried
BUTTERNUT SQUASH SOUP

SERVES 4

BUTTERNUT SQUASH IS HEALTHY COMFORT FOOD at its best! Simmer it in a soup on your induction cooktop for spoonfuls of guilt-free goodness. If you can find butternut squash that has already been peeled and chopped in the produce section of the grocery store, use it. If not, be sure to use a sharp knife to remove the skin from your squash.

In a large ferrous-bottomed soup pot or Dutch oven, heat the butter over medium-high heat (300°F). Add the onion, celery, carrot, and curry powder. Cook, stirring occasionally, until the vegetables begin to soften, about 5 minutes.

Raise the temperature to high (450°F) and add the squash, apple, and broth. When the soup comes to a boil, reduce the heat to low (180°F) and cook, covered, until the squash is very tender, about 30 minutes.

Use an immersion blender to puree the soup, or work in batches and puree the soup in a standing blender. Stir in the lemon juice. Taste and adjust the seasonings, adding salt and freshly ground black pepper to taste. Top each serving with 1½ teaspoons of yogurt and 1½ teaspoons of pumpkin seeds. Garnish with the fresh thyme (if using).

2 tablespoons unsalted butter

1 small onion, chopped

1 rib celery, chopped

1 carrot, peeled and chopped

2 teaspoons curry powder

1 butternut squash, seeded, peeled, and coarsely chopped (about 6 cups)

1 large tart green apple, peeled, cored, and coarsely chopped (about 2 cups)

4 cups chicken broth

Juice of ½ lemon

Salt and freshly ground black pepper

2 tablespoons plain yogurt

2 tablespoons toasted pumpkin seeds

4 sprigs fresh thyme (optional)

Crunchy
QUINOA SALAD

SERVES
6

THIS EASY-TO-ASSEMBLE GRAIN SALAD is a super portable lunch or dish to bring to a picnic. Packed with crisp vegetables, it's a refreshing alternative to lettuce-based salad combinations. Between the quinoa and all the veggies, it's also a good source of fiber to keep you feeling fuller longer!

1 cup quinoa

2 cups water

⅓ cup olive oil

Juice of 1 lemon

1 teaspoon ground cumin

1 teaspoon salt, plus more to taste

¼ teaspoon red pepper flakes

1 cup halved cherry tomatoes

1 cup sugar snap peas, coarsely chopped

½ cup sliced radishes

1 can (15 ounces) chickpeas, drained and rinsed

4 green onions, finely chopped

¼ cup chopped fresh parsley

Freshly ground black pepper

Bring the quinoa and water to a boil in a ferrous-bottomed saucepan over high heat (450°F). Reduce the heat to medium-low (180°F), cover, and simmer until the quinoa is tender and the water has been absorbed, 10 to 15 minutes. Set aside to cool.

In a large bowl, whisk together the olive oil, lemon juice, cumin, 1 teaspoon salt, and red pepper flakes. Add the quinoa, tomatoes, snap peas, radishes, chickpeas, and green onions; toss until the mixture is evenly combined. Stir in the parsley; season to taste with salt and pepper. Serve at room temperature or chilled.

French Potato-
GREEN BEAN SALAD

SERVES
6

POTATO SALADS GO WAY BEYOND TRADITIONAL, mayo-laden versions! This tasty recipe comes
together easily on your induction cooktop and uses Asian fish sauce, a common ingredient in
Thai cooking. It makes a great substitute for anchovies that's easy to have on hand.

Fill a large ferrous-bottomed pot with well-salted water and bring
to a boil over high heat (450°F). Add the potatoes and bay leaf. Reduce
the heat to medium (240°F) so the water is at a brisk simmer. Cook
until the potatoes are firm but easily pierced with a fork, about
15 minutes. Add the beans in the last 3 minutes of cooking time.
Drain the vegetables and transfer to a large bowl. Remove the bay leaf.

While the potatoes are cooking, make the vinaigrette. In a small bowl,
combine the garlic, fish sauce, capers, mustard, and vinegar. Slowly
whisk in the olive oil. Season to taste with salt and pepper. Toss the
potatoes and green beans with the dressing. Serve on a bed of arugula
topped with fresh parsley.

Salt

1½ pounds baby potatoes

1 bay leaf

1 pound green beans

3 cloves garlic, minced

1 tablespoon fish sauce

1 tablespoon capers

2 teaspoons Dijon mustard

3 tablespoons white wine vinegar

⅓ cup extra virgin olive oil

Freshly ground black pepper

8 ounces arugula

¼ cup chopped fresh parsley

Pesto TORTELLINI SALAD

SERVES
2

BEYOND THE FACT THAT THIS DISH RELIES ON ONLY A FEW main ingredients, the true beauty of this recipe is that you can cook the tortellini and broccoli together in the same pot. If you're packing it for lunch, make it the night before. The flavors will only improve with time.

Salt

½ pound fresh tortellini

3 cups broccoli florets, cut into walnut-size pieces

¼ cup prepared pesto

1 roasted pepper, chopped

12 grape tomatoes, halved

2 tablespoons grated Parmesan

Fill a large ferrous-bottomed pot with cold water, add a generous pinch of salt, and bring the water to a boil over high heat (450°F). Add the tortellini and cook according to package instructions. In the last 2 minutes of cooking time, add the broccoli. Reserve ¼ cup of the cooking liquid and drain the pasta and broccoli.

In a large bowl, combine the pasta, broccoli, pesto, pepper, and tomatoes. Toss gently to coat, adding the reserved cooking water if necessary, a tablespoon at a time, to ensure the sauce is smooth and even. Sprinkle with the Parmesan and refrigerate until ready to serve.

Asparagus–
FARRO SALAD

IF YOU'VE NEVER TRIED FARRO, IT'S TIME for a treat! Farro is especially well suited to grain salads because it retains its texture even when cooked. But there are so many ways to enjoy it cooked on your induction burner—simply substitute farro for rice in your favorite recipes.

Salt

1½ cups semi-pearled farro

1 bunch asparagus, trimmed, cut into 1½-inch lengths

1 red bell pepper, cored, seeded, and chopped

½ cup small red onion, finely chopped

3 tablespoons chopped fresh dill or 1 tablespoon dried

½ cup olive oil

¼ cup red wine vinegar

Freshly ground black pepper

1 bag (5 ounces) baby arugula

1 package (5 ounces) crumbled feta cheese

Fill a large ferrous-bottomed pot with cold water, add a generous pinch of salt, and bring the water to a boil over high heat (450°F). Add the farro, reduce the heat to medium-low (180°F), and cook, covered, until tender, about 30 minutes. Drain the farro and transfer to a large bowl.

Bring 2 cups of water to a boil in the same pot over high heat (450°F). Add a generous pinch of salt along with the asparagus. Cook, partially covered, for 3 minutes, until the asparagus is crisp-tender. Drain the asparagus and add it to the bowl along with the bell pepper and red onion.

In a small bowl, whisk together the dill, olive oil, and vinegar. Season to taste with salt and pepper. Pour the dressing over the farro mixture and toss until the ingredients are thoroughly coated. Serve the salad on a bed of arugula with the feta scattered on top.

Sicilian
CAULIFLOWER SALAD

SERVES
4

GET RAW VEGETABLES THAT ARE CRISP-TENDER and able to absorb flavorings easily without blanching! Simply allow the vegetables to absorb flavor as they slowly cool. This recipe works just as well with broccoli if you prefer that in place of the cauliflower.

Bring a large, ferrous-bottomed pot of lightly salted water to a boil over high heat (450°F). Add the cauliflower and cook for 1 minute until crisp-tender. Drain well and transfer the florets to a large bowl. Add the olive oil, vinegar, garlic, oregano, pepper flakes, chickpeas, olives, bell pepper, onion, tomatoes, and parsley. Toss well until thoroughly combined.

Cover with plastic wrap and let sit for 30 minutes before serving. Alternatively, refrigerate overnight and bring to room temperature before serving.

Salt

1 head cauliflower, chopped into bite-size florets

½ cup olive oil

3 tablespoons red wine vinegar

3 cloves garlic, minced

½ teaspoon dried oregano

½ teaspoon red pepper flakes

1 can (15 ounces) chickpeas, rinsed and drained

½ cup chopped green olives

½ red bell pepper, chopped

½ small red onion, halved and sliced

¼ cup julienned sun-dried tomatoes

¼ cup chopped fresh parsley

SPINACH SALAD
with Hot Bacon Dressing

ORIGINALLY THIS RECIPE MAY HAVE OFFERED FRUGAL cooks a way to use up leftover bacon drippings, but it has certainly endured for an obvious reason—it's delicious! Hint: Slightly older eggs work better than super-fresh eggs in this case because they are easier to peel.

Place the eggs in a small ferrous-bottomed pot and cover with cold water by at least 1 inch. Bring the water to a boil over high heat (450°F), then place the pot on a heatproof surface.

Leave the eggs in the hot water for 15 minutes, then transfer them to a bowl of cold water. When the eggs are cool enough to handle, peel off the shells. Slice each egg into 8 pieces and set aside.

While the eggs are cooking, fry the bacon in a ferrous-bottomed skillet over medium heat (240°F) and remove to a paper towel to drain, reserving 3 tablespoons of the rendered fat. Turn off the induction cooktop. Crumble the bacon and set aside.

Add the red wine vinegar, sugar, and mustard to the skillet with the reserved bacon fat and whisk until smooth. Season to taste with salt and pepper.

In a large bowl, combine the mushrooms, onion, and spinach. Add the dressing and bacon and toss until thoroughly coated. Divide the salad between 4 plates or bowls and top with equal portions of egg slices.

2 eggs

8 slices bacon

3 tablespoons red wine vinegar

1 teaspoon sugar

½ teaspoon Dijon mustard

Salt and freshly ground black pepper

4 large mushrooms

1 small red onion, sliced

8 ounces baby spinach

Chapter 4

DINNERS
+SIDES

Penne with
BOLOGNESE SAUCE

THE BEST BOLOGNESE FLAVOR COMES FROM a long, low simmer—which is easy to achieve with your induction cooktop! Use a food processor to make quick prep work for this dish. You can chop the onions, celery, carrots, and garlic in one fell swoop.

2 tablespoons unsalted butter

2 tablespoons olive oil

1 medium onion, finely chopped

1 rib celery, finely chopped

1 large carrot, peeled and finely chopped

4 cloves garlic, minced

¼ pound bacon, chopped

1 pound lean ground beef

¾ pound ground pork

1 tablespoon dried oregano

1 teaspoon salt

½ teaspoon black pepper

1 teaspoon rubbed sage

½ teaspoon red pepper flakes

¼ teaspoon ground nutmeg

1 cup dry white wine

1 cup beef broth

1 can (28 ounces) crushed tomatoes

½ cup heavy cream

½ cup grated Parmesan

1 pound penne, cooked according to package directions

2 tablespoons fresh oregano

In a ferrous-bottomed Dutch oven, heat the butter and olive oil over medium heat (240°F) until the butter begins to foam. Add the onion, celery, carrot, garlic, and bacon. Cook, stirring occasionally, until the onions are translucent, 8 to 10 minutes.

Add the beef and pork, and cook, breaking up the meat with the side of a spoon as it cooks, until browned. Add the oregano, salt, pepper, sage, red pepper flakes, and nutmeg and cook for 2 to 3 minutes to allow the flavors to combine. Increase the heat to medium-high (330°F) and add the wine and beef broth. Cook, stirring occasionally, until the mixture is almost dry.

Add the tomatoes and bring the sauce to a boil, then reduce the heat to low (150°F) and simmer, partially uncovered, for about 3 hours, stirring occasionally to prevent sticking.

About 10 minutes before serving, stir in the cream and Parmesan. Toss with the penne and top with the oregano before serving.

Skillet
LASAGNA

WANT HOMEMADE LASAGNA ON THE TABLE IN ABOUT HALF THE TIME it takes to bake it the traditional way? No-boil lasagna noodles are a true time-saver in the kitchen. Paired with your induction cooktop, they'll have you enjoying yummy lasagna in so much less time!

¾ pound lean ground beef

2 cloves garlic, minced

1 can (14.5 ounces) diced tomatoes with basil, oregano, and garlic, undrained

1 jar (28 ounces) spaghetti sauce

⅔ cup condensed cream of onion soup, undiluted

2 large eggs, lightly beaten

1¼ cups 1% cottage cheese

¾ teaspoon Italian seasoning

9 no-boil lasagna noodles

½ cup shredded Monterey Jack cheese

½ cup shredded mozzarella cheese

In a large, ferrous-bottomed skillet, cook the beef and garlic over medium heat (270°F), breaking up the meat with the side of a spoon as it cooks, until the meat is no longer pink, about 10 minutes. Add the tomatoes and spaghetti sauce and stir until thoroughly combined. Turn off the cooktop and transfer the meat mixture to a large bowl; set aside.

In a small bowl, combine the soup, eggs, cottage cheese, and Italian seasoning.

Spread 1 cup of the meat sauce in the bottom of the skillet, followed by 1 cup of the cottage cheese mixture. Spread half of the noodles over the top, breaking them to fit as needed. Repeat the layers of cottage cheese mixture, meat sauce, and noodles. Top with the remaining meat sauce. Place the lasagna over medium-high heat (300°F). When the sauce begins to boil, reduce the heat to medium-low (180°F) and simmer, covered, until the noodles are tender, 15 to 17 minutes.

Remove the lasagna from the cooktop and set on a heatproof surface. Sprinkle the Monterey Jack and mozzarella on top. Cover and let stand until the cheeses are melted, 2 to 3 minutes.

BEEF STROGANOFF
Over Noodles

**SERVES
4**

THIS RICH, CREAMY DISH IS CONSIDERED A CLASSIC in Russian cuisine, but its hearty flavor makes it a true international favorite. It is ideally suited to induction cooking because it requires several important temperature changes along the way.

In a ferrous-bottom skillet over medium heat (240°F), melt 2 tablespoons of the butter. Cook the mushrooms, onions, and garlic, stirring occasionally, until the onions are tender, about 5 minutes. Transfer the vegetables to a bowl and set aside.

In the same skillet, cook the beef, stirring occasionally, until browned. Stir in 1 cup of the broth, the salt, and the Worcestershire sauce. Increase the heat to medium-high (330°F). When the liquid comes to a boil, reduce the heat to medium-low (180°F). Cover and simmer for 15 minutes.

In a small bowl, whisk the remaining ½ cup broth into the flour, then stir the flour mixture into the beef mixture. Add the reserved vegetables. Raise the heat to medium-high (330°F) and cook, stirring constantly. When the mixture begins to boil, cook 1 minute longer. Turn off the cooktop and stir in the sour cream until thoroughly combined. Serve over the cooked egg noodles.

¼ cup unsalted butter, divided

1 package (8 ounces) sliced brown mushrooms

2 medium onions, thinly sliced

1 clove garlic, minced

1½ pounds beef sirloin, sliced into 1½ x ½-inch strips

1½ cups beef broth, divided

½ teaspoon salt

1 teaspoon Worcestershire sauce

¼ cup all-purpose flour

1½ cups sour cream

3 cups cooked egg noodles, prepared according to package directions

One-Pan
SWEDISH MEATBALLS

SERVES 8

MAKING SWEDISH MEATBELLS JUST GOT EASIER! Lingonberry jelly, the traditional accompaniment, is sometimes difficult to find, but a spoonful of cranberry jelly works in its place quite nicely. Of course, these meatballs are perfectly delicious even without the jelly, so you'll hardly be disappointed if you omit this ingredient altogether.

Tear the bread into a few large pieces and set in a large bowl. Pour the milk over the bread and let sit about 15 minutes.

Meanwhile, in a large, heavy, ferrous-bottomed skillet, melt 2 tablespoons of the butter over medium heat (240°F). Add the onion and cook until translucent, 3 to 4 minutes. Transfer the onion to a small bowl and set aside to cool. Turn off the cooktop.

Use a fork to beat the soaked bread into a thick paste. Add the cooked onions, eggs, ground pork, ground beef, salt, pepper, nutmeg, and cardamom. Use your clean hands to mix everything together until thoroughly combined. Form the meatballs about 1 inch thick and place them on a plate or sheet pan.

In the same skillet, heat 3 tablespoons of butter over medium heat (240°F). Working in batches, cook the meatballs until browned, 5 to 7 minutes. Transfer the browned meatballs to a plate as you add new ones to the skillet. When all the meatballs are browned, add the remaining 3 tablespoons butter and the flour to the skillet. Whisk until the butter has melted and the flour mixture is smooth. Continue to cook, stirring occasionally, until the flour is light brown. Slowly whisk in the broth until smooth. Return the meatballs to the skillet and reduce the heat to medium-low (180°F). Cook, covered, until the meatballs are cooked through, about 10 minutes.

Transfer the meatballs to a serving dish. Stir the sour cream and jelly (if using) into the remaining sauce and pour over the meatballs. Top with the parsley just before serving.

5 slices bread, crusts removed

⅔ cup milk

8 tablespoons unsalted butter, divided

1 large yellow or white onion, grated

2 eggs

1 pound ground pork

1½ pounds ground beef

2 teaspoons kosher salt

2 teaspoons freshly ground black pepper

1 teaspoon ground nutmeg

1 teaspoon ground cardamom

⅓ cup all-purpose flour

4 cups beef broth

½ cup sour cream

2 tablespoons cranberry jelly (optional)

2 tablespoons chopped fresh parsley

Stuffed
CABBAGE

THIS COMFORT-FOOD RECIPE REALLY SATISFIES! A half-pint of leftover takeout rice is a handy shortcut for making these delicious cabbage rolls, an Eastern European delicacy. Serve with mashed potatoes and a salad of cucumbers and onions.

8 large cabbage leaves

1 pound lean ground beef

1 cup cooked white rice

¼ cup chopped onion

1 egg, slightly beaten

1 teaspoon salt

¼ teaspoon ground black pepper

1 can (10.75 ounces) condensed tomato soup, divided

1 cup water

Bring a large, wide ferrous-bottomed saucepan of lightly salted water to a boil over high heat (450°F). Add the cabbage leaves a few at a time and cook until softened, 2 to 4 minutes. Transfer the cooked cabbage leaves to a large bowl and continue until all the cabbage is cooked. When the leaves are cool enough to handle, use a paring knife to carefully trim the rib from the bottom so that each leaf is an even thickness.

In a medium mixing bowl, combine the ground beef, rice, onion, egg, salt, pepper, and 2 tablespoons of the tomato soup. Use your clean hands to mix everything together until thoroughly combined. Divide the beef mixture into 8 equal portions and form each into an egg shape.

To assemble, spread a cabbage leaf on a flat surface and set a piece of the beef filling in the center near the bottom of the leaf. Fold in the sides and gently roll up the leaf, securing it with a toothpick if necessary. Repeat with the remaining ingredients.

Arrange the rolls, seam-side down, in a large, ferrous-bottomed skillet and pour the remaining tomato soup and water over the top. Bring the liquid to a boil over medium-high heat (350°F). Reduce the heat to medium-low (180°F) and simmer, covered, for about 40 minutes, basting occasionally with the liquid, until the cabbage leaves are very tender.

PAN-SEARED STEAKS
with Red Wine Sauce

SERVES
4

GET STEAKHOUSE FLAVOR WITH THE HELP of your induction burner! For best results, make sure your steaks are at room temperature before cooking them. Simply season them and let them sit on the counter for about half an hour or so before you begin.

Pat the steaks dry and season generously with salt and black pepper.

Heat 1 tablespoon of the oil in a large, ferrous-bottomed skillet over high heat (420°F). Cook the steaks in 2 batches, turning once, to the desired doneness, about 4 minutes per side for medium-rare. Transfer the steaks to a large plate and cover loosely with foil. Drain the skillet, but do not wipe it out.

In the same skillet, warm the remaining 1 tablespoon oil over medium-high heat (360°F) and cook the garlic and shallot until pale golden, about 30 seconds. Add the wine and boil, stirring and scraping up any brown bits, until reduced by half, 2 to 3 minutes. Add the water, soy sauce, and any meat juices from the plate and boil until reduced by half, 3 to 4 minutes.

Reduce the heat to medium-low (180°F) and whisk in the butter, 1 piece at a time, until the sauce is slightly thickened. Taste and adjust the seasonings. Stir in the parsley and pour the sauce over the steaks before serving.

4 (½-inch-thick) boneless rib-eye steaks (2 pounds)

Salt and freshly ground black pepper

2 tablespoons vegetable oil, divided

2 cloves garlic, finely chopped

1 shallot, finely chopped

¾ cup dry red wine

¼ cup water

1½ teaspoons soy sauce

3 tablespoons unsalted butter, cut into 3 pieces

1 tablespoon chopped flat-leaf parsley

Slow-Cooked
BEEF STEW

SERVES
6

DID YOU KNOW YOUR INDUCTION COOKTOP can perform double duty as a slow cooker? All you need is a cast-iron Dutch oven with a tight-fitting lid. Best of all, with this configuration you can brown your meat directly in the same pot without dirtying another skillet.

2 pounds boneless beef chuck, cut into 1-inch cubes

¼ cup all-purpose flour

1 teaspoon salt

½ teaspoon freshly ground black pepper

2 tablespoons olive oil

1 large onion, chopped

3 cloves garlic, minced

1 teaspoon dried thyme

1 can (28 ounces) crushed tomatoes

2 cups beef broth

1 bay leaf

1 tablespoon Worcestershire sauce

3 large carrots, peeled and coarsely chopped

2 large russet potatoes, peeled and coarsely chopped

1 cup frozen peas

¼ cup chopped fresh parsley

In a large bowl, combine the beef, flour, salt, and pepper. Toss to coat.

In a cast-iron Dutch oven over high heat (390°F), warm the olive oil. Sear the beef, in batches if necessary, until browned on all sides, about 5 minutes. Add the onion, garlic, and thyme, and cook until the onion begins to soften, about 5 minutes longer. Add the tomatoes, broth, bay leaf, and Worcestershire sauce. When the mixture comes to a boil, reduce the heat to medium-low (180°F) and add the carrots and potatoes.

Cover and cook until the beef is fork-tender, about 4 hours. Remove from the cooktop and add the peas. Let stand, uncovered, until the peas are thawed, about 10 minutes. Remove the bay leaf and stir in the parsley just before serving.

Perfect
POT ROAST

YOU DON'T NEED TO WAIT FOR A SUNDAY DINNER to enjoy this delicious one-pot meal! It needs very little attention as it slow cooks on your induction burner. Serve with crusty bread and a side salad for a simple but satisfying meal.

Pat the roast dry with a paper towel and sprinkle with the pepper and 1½ teaspoons of the salt. In a ferrous-bottomed Dutch oven over medium-high heat (330°F), heat the oil. Sear the roast on all sides. Transfer the roast to a plate and set aside.

In the same pot, add the onions, celery, and remaining ½ teaspoon salt. Reduce the heat to medium (240°F) and cook, stirring occasionally, until the onions are browned, 8 to 10 minutes. Add the garlic, tomato paste, thyme, and bay leaves and cook 1 minute longer.

Add the wine, stirring to loosen any browned bits from the pot; stir in the broth. Return the roast to the pot. Arrange the potatoes, parsnips, and carrots around the roast. When the liquid begins to boil, reduce the heat to medium-low (180°F) and cook, covered, until the meat is fork-tender, 2 to 2½ hours.

Transfer the roast and vegetables to a serving dish and cover loosely with foil to keep warm. Discard the bay leaves and skim the fat from the cooking juices. Raise the heat to high (420°F) and cook the liquid that remains until it is reduced by half (about 1½ cups), 10 to 12 minutes. Stir in the vinegar and parsley. Taste and adjust the seasonings. Serve the roast and vegetables with the sauce on the side.

1 boneless beef chuck roast
(3 to 4 pounds)

2 teaspoons freshly ground black
pepper, plus more as needed

2 teaspoons salt, divided,
plus more as needed

2 tablespoons olive oil

2 medium onions, cut into 1-inch pieces

2 ribs celery, chopped

3 cloves garlic, minced

1 tablespoon tomato paste

1 teaspoon dried thyme

2 bay leaves

1 cup dry red wine or
reduced-sodium beef broth

2 cups reduced-sodium beef broth

1 pound small red potatoes, quartered

4 medium parsnips, peeled
and cut into 2-inch pieces

6 medium carrots, peeled
and cut into 2-inch pieces

1 tablespoon red wine vinegar

2 tablespoons chopped fresh parsley

Salisbury
STEAK

IT'S EASY TO DRESS UP AN ORDINARY package of ground beef! Just turn to your induction cooktop and this simple recipe can be on your table in less than 30 minutes. Salisbury steak is best served over mashed potatoes, although egg noodles are another good option if you prefer them instead.

1 can (10.5 ounces) condensed French onion soup, undiluted, divided

1½ pounds lean ground beef

½ cup dry bread crumbs

1 egg

¼ teaspoon salt

⅛ teaspoon freshly ground black pepper

1 tablespoon olive oil

8 ounces sliced brown mushrooms, coarsely chopped

1 tablespoon all-purpose flour

¼ cup ketchup

¼ cup water

1 tablespoon Worcestershire sauce

½ teaspoon mustard powder

In a large bowl, combine ⅓ cup of the soup with the ground beef, bread crumbs, egg, salt, and black pepper. Mix until thoroughly combined, and then shape into 6 oval patties.

In a large ferrous-bottomed skillet over medium-high heat (360°F), heat the oil. Cook the patties and mushrooms until browned, turning the patties once, 5 to 7 minutes.

Meanwhile, in a small bowl, whisk together the flour and remaining soup. Add the ketchup, water, Worcestershire sauce, and mustard powder and stir until thoroughly combined. Pour the sauce over the meat. When the sauce begins to boil, reduce the heat to medium-low (210°F), cover, and cook, stirring occasionally, until the patties are cooked through and the sauce thickens, about 20 minutes.

Quick & Easy
MONGOLIAN BEEF

SERVES 4

YOU CAN HAVE THIS FAVORITE CHINESE TAKEOUT dish on the table in less time than it takes to have it delivered—with just a little bit of planning. If you have a steel wok that passes the magnet test, use it. However, an ordinary induction-ready skillet will work just as well. Because stir-fries require a very short cooking time, be sure to have all your ingredients measured and ready before you begin.

Combine the beef, sesame oil, 2 teaspoons of the soy sauce, and 1 tablespoon of the cornstarch in a large bowl. Toss to combine. Cover and refrigerate for at least an hour or up to 8 hours. Just before you're ready to start cooking, dredge the beef in 4 tablespoons cornstarch until lightly coated. In a small bowl, combine the remaining 1 tablespoon cornstarch and water. Stir until thoroughly mixed. Set aside.

In a large, ferrous-bottomed skillet or wok over high heat (450°F), heat the vegetable oil. Cook the beef, stirring constantly, until browned, 2 to 3 minutes. Transfer the beef to a plate. Drain the skillet or wok, reserving about 1 tablespoon of oil in the skillet.

Reduce the heat to medium-high (360°F). Add the ginger and chili-garlic paste and cook, stirring constantly, until fragrant, about 15 seconds, and then add the garlic. Cook, stirring frequently, for another 10 seconds and then add the remaining ⅓ cup soy sauce and the chicken broth. When the liquid begins to boil, add the brown sugar and stir until dissolved.

Slowly stir in the cornstarch-water mixture and cook until the sauce thickens, about 2 minutes. Add the reserved beef and the scallions and toss until warmed through, about 30 seconds. Serve with the rice.

1 pound flank steak, sliced against the grain into ¼-inch-thick slices

2 teaspoons sesame oil

2 teaspoons plus ⅓ cup reduced-sodium soy sauce, divided

6 tablespoons cornstarch, divided

1 tablespoon water

2 tablespoons vegetable oil

1 tablespoon grated fresh ginger

1 tablespoon chili-garlic paste

4 cloves garlic, finely chopped

⅓ cup reduced-sodium chicken broth

3 tablespoons brown sugar

2 small bunches scallions, cut into 1-inch-long slices on the diagonal

4 cups cooked brown rice

Asian-Style
BEEF LETTUCE WRAPS

THESE EASY-TO-ASSEMBLE LETTUCE WRAPS are a refreshing alternative to the usual stir-fry and rice combinations if you're trying to eat fewer carbs. But if mu shu pancakes are more to your liking, you can add 2 cups of shredded broccoli or cabbage to the mix and enjoy this tasty beef dish wrapped in flour tortillas instead. This recipe is flexible, just like your induction burner!

1 tablespoon sesame oil

1 pound lean ground beef

1 large onion, chopped

1 large carrot, peeled and grated

½ red bell pepper, chopped

¼ cup hoisin sauce

2 cloves garlic, minced

1 tablespoon reduced-sodium soy sauce

1 tablespoon rice wine vinegar

1 can (8 ounces) water chestnuts, drained and finely chopped

1 bunch scallions, chopped

16 Boston Bibb or butter lettuce leaves

¼ cup chopped peanuts

In a large ferrous-bottomed skillet or wok, heat the oil over medium-high heat (360°F). Cook the beef, breaking up the meat with the side of a spoon as it cooks, until browned, 5 to 7 minutes. Transfer the beef to a bowl.

In the same skillet, add the onion, carrot, and bell pepper. Cook, stirring constantly, until the vegetables begin to soften, 3 to 5 minutes. Add the hoisin sauce, garlic, soy sauce, and vinegar. Stir until thoroughly combined. Add the water chestnuts, scallions, and the reserved beef. Cook, stirring constantly, until the scallions soften, about 2 minutes. To serve, spoon the meat mixture into the lettuce leaves and top with the peanuts.

FETTUCINE *Carbonara*

MULTIPLE POTS ON A SINGLE COOKING SURFACE? NO PROBLEM! Remember that your induction burner makes fast work of things. You'll see how easy it can be to boil some noodles and make a quick sauce—all with one burner! For best results, use dried pasta (not fresh).

1¼ teaspoons salt, divided

1 pound fettuccine

4 slices bacon, chopped

2 tablespoons unsalted butter

2 cloves garlic, minced

3 large eggs, lightly beaten

½ cup half-and-half

⅓ cup grated Parmesan

2 tablespoons chopped fresh parsley

Fill a ferrous-bottomed soup pot with water, add 1 teaspoon of the salt, and bring to a rolling boil over high heat (450°F). Add the pasta and stir gently to ensure the noodles are completely covered. When the water begins to boil again, remove the pot from the heat and set on a heatproof surface. Cover and let sit according to the time indicated on the package directions (usually 8 to 10 minutes).

Meanwhile, reduce the heat to medium (240°F) and place the bacon in a large, cold ferrous-bottomed skillet. Cook, stirring occasionally, for 4 to 5 minutes, until the bacon is browned. Use tongs to transfer the bacon to a plate lined with paper towels. When cool enough to handle, crumble the bacon. Drain the bacon grease and add the butter and garlic to the skillet. Cook until the garlic is fragrant, about 1 minute. Turn off the heat until the pasta is ready to be drained.

Drain the pasta when it is "al dente," reserving ½ cup of the cooking water. Use a fork to beat the eggs and remaining ¼ teaspoon salt in a medium bowl, adding the reserved pasta water slowly in a steady stream to temper the eggs. Turn the heat to medium-high (300°F) and add the pasta to the skillet along with the half-and-half and the egg mixture. Toss gently until the sauce thickens and clings to the pasta, 1 to 2 minutes. Add the Parmesan and bacon; continue tossing until thoroughly combined. Sprinkle the parsley on top just before serving.

Sausage & Shrimp
JAMBALAYA

SERVES
6

YOUR INDUCTION COOKTOP WILL PROVIDE the long, slow cooking time this easy one-pot meal needs to develop maximum flavor. Don't let the long list of ingredients deter you! One bite will transport you to New Orleans faster than you can say, *"Laissez les bon temps rouler."*

In a ferrous-bottomed Dutch oven over medium-high (300°F) heat, warm the olive oil and cook the sausage, onion, bell pepper, celery, and garlic until the vegetables are tender, 5 to 7 minutes. Add the thyme, cayenne, tomatoes, tomato sauce, chicken broth, and bay leaf.

When the mixture comes to a boil, add the rice and reduce the heat to medium-low (180°F). Cover and let the mixture simmer for 20 minutes. Add the shrimp and cook until pink, another 5 to 7 minutes. Season to taste with salt and pepper. Garnish with the parsley. Remove the bay leaf before serving with the hot sauce on the side (if using).

1 tablespoon olive oil

12 ounces andouille sausage, cut into ¼-inch slices

1 small onion, chopped

1 red bell pepper, cored, seeded, and chopped

1 rib celery, chopped

2 cloves garlic, minced

½ teaspoon dried thyme

½ teaspoon cayenne pepper

1 can (14 ounces) diced tomatoes

1 can (8 ounces) tomato sauce

2½ cups chicken broth

1 bay leaf

1 cup long-grain rice

¾ pound medium fresh shrimp, peeled and deveined

Salt and freshly ground black pepper

2 tablespoons chopped fresh parsley

Hot sauce (optional)

PORK TERIYAKI *with*
Grilled Pineapple & Peppers

YES! YOU CAN USE YOUR INDUCTION COOKTOP to make grilled dishes like this sweet-and-salty classic. However, make sure you use your ventilation hood and watch your dish carefully because sugar can burn quickly and generate a fair amount of smoke. Serve with rice and steamed broccoli.

¾ cup reduced-sodium soy sauce

2 tablespoons brown sugar

2 teaspoons grated fresh ginger

2 cloves garlic, minced

1 tablespoon sesame oil

2 pounds boneless pork chops

1 tablespoon sesame seeds

1 fresh pineapple, cored and sliced

1 red bell pepper, cored, seeded, and quartered

In a small bowl, combine the soy sauce, brown sugar, ginger, garlic, and sesame oil. Place ½ cup of the soy sauce mixture in a resealable plastic bag and add the pork chops. Cover the remaining soy mixture to use when grilling the pork. Refrigerate the pork chops for at least 4 hours, preferably overnight.

Remove the pork chops from the marinade and pat dry with a paper towel. In a ferrous-bottomed grill pan over high heat (420°F), grill the pork for 3 to 5 minutes per side, basting frequently with the reserved sauce, until a thermometer inserted into the thickest part of the chop registers 145°F. Transfer the chops to a plate and sprinkle with the sesame seeds. Cover loosely to keep warm.

Grill the pineapple slices and bell pepper, flipping occasionally to avoid burning, until tender, 3 to 5 minutes. Serve the pork with the grilled pineapple and pepper.

Italian
SAUSAGE & PEPPERS

**SERVES
4**

THERE ARE SO MANY WAYS TO ENJOY this hearty Italian-American classic! It works well in sandwich rolls or with pasta, but you can try it with polenta or mashed potatoes for a gluten-free option. Whichever way you serve them, these sausages are sure to make your family-favorites list.

In a large ferrous-bottomed skillet over medium-high heat (330°F), warm the olive oil and cook the sausages, turning occasionally, until browned on all sides and cooked through, 8 to 10 minutes. Remove the sausages to a plate.

In the same skillet, add the onion, peppers, and garlic. Cook, stirring occasionally, until the vegetables soften, 8 to 10 minutes. Add the wine and scrape the bottom of the skillet to loosen any browned bits. Cook until the liquid evaporates. Add the oregano, red pepper flakes (if using), tomatoes, and sugar. Stir until thoroughly combined.

Slice the sausages as you like and return them to the skillet. Reduce the heat to medium-low (180°F) and simmer, partially covered, for 30 minutes, until the sauce thickens. Season to taste with salt and pepper. Serve topped with the parsley.

1 tablespoon olive oil

1 pound Italian sausage

1 large onion, halved and sliced

2 bell peppers, cored, seeded, and sliced

4 cloves garlic, chopped

¼ cup red wine

1 teaspoon dried oregano

¼ teaspoon red pepper flakes (optional)

1 can (28 ounces) crushed tomatoes

1 tablespoon sugar

Salt and freshly ground black pepper

2 tablespoons chopped fresh parsley

PULLED PORK
with Root Beer Barbecue Sauce

PULLED PORK IS A DELICIOUS FIX-IT AND FORGET-IT type of dish that feeds a hungry crowd easily. And with this recipe you can enjoy a lot of subtle flavor by using root beer as a base for your barbecue sauce.

Use paper towels to pat the roast dry. Season generously with salt and pepper.

In a ferrous-bottomed Dutch oven, heat the oil over high heat (450°F). Cook the pork roast until browned on all sides, 6 to 10 minutes. Add the onion, garlic, bay leaf, and root beer. Reduce the heat to medium-low (180°F) and cook, covered, until the pork is fork-tender, 4 to 5 hours. Transfer the pork to a rimmed baking sheet and cover loosely with foil. Let rest for about 30 minutes. Discard the bay leaf.

Meanwhile, skim the fat from the cooking liquid and then add the barbecue sauce. Cook over medium-high heat, uncovered, stirring occasionally, until the mixture is thick and glossy, 8 to 10 minutes.

When the meat is cool enough to handle, use 2 forks to pull the pork apart. Combine the shredded meat and the barbecue sauce mixture, tossing gently until thoroughly coated. To serve, spoon about ½ cup pork mixture into each bun and top with ¼ cup coleslaw (if using).

1 boneless pork loin roast (about 3 pounds)

Salt and freshly ground black pepper

1 tablespoon olive oil

1 large onion, chopped

4 cloves garlic, chopped

1 bay leaf

1 can (12 ounces) root beer

1 jar (12 ounces) barbecue sauce

12 sandwich rolls

3 cups coleslaw (optional)

PORK TENDERLOIN
with Sun-Dried Tomatoes & Kale

YOU DON'T NEED AN OVEN TO ENJOY flavor-packed pork tenderloin. Take it stovetop by slicing it into medallions! Another benefit of slicing it before you cook it? You're essentially creating more surface area in which to develop a delicious, crispy coating.

1¼ pounds pork tenderloin, trimmed and cut into 12 medallions

Salt and freshly ground black pepper

1 tablespoon olive oil

6 cloves garlic, thinly sliced

1 small onion, thinly sliced

¼ teaspoon red pepper flakes

5 cups curly kale (about 2 bunches), tough ribs removed and chopped into 2-inch pieces

1 cup reduced-sodium chicken broth

½ cup oil-packed sun-dried tomatoes, coarsely chopped

¼ cup grated Parmesan

Dry the pork with a paper towel and season with salt and pepper. In a large ferrous-bottomed skillet, heat the oil over medium-high heat (330°F). Add the tenderloin medallions to the skillet and cook until browned on one side, 2 to 3 minutes. Flip and brown on the opposite sides, another 2 to 3 minutes. Transfer the tenderloin to a plate, cover to keep warm, and set aside.

Reduce the heat to medium (240°F). Add the garlic and cook until it is golden brown, about 2 minutes. Add the onion, red pepper flakes, and kale and cook, stirring constantly, until the kale starts to wilt, about 1 minute. Add the chicken broth and cook, partially covered, until almost all the liquid has evaporated or been absorbed, about 4 minutes. Stir in the tomatoes and cook until the kale is tender, about 1 minute longer. Divide the kale among 4 plates, arrange the tenderloin pieces on top, and serve sprinkled with the Parmesan.

SMOTHERED PORK CHOPS
with Cabbage & Apples

SERVES
4

THIS LONG, SLOW COOKING METHOD IS GUARANTEED to render your pork chops tender and delicious without a lot of fuss on your part. Serve over mashed potatoes or rice, whichever you prefer.

Season the pork chops with the Cajun seasoning. Lightly dredge in the flour.

Heat the olive oil in a large ferrous-bottomed Dutch oven or heavy pot over medium-high heat (360°F). Add the pork chops 2 at a time, and cook until lightly browned, about 2 minutes per side. Remove the pork chops and transfer to a platter. Repeat with the remaining pork chops and set aside.

In the same pot, add the apples and onion. Cook, stirring occasionally, until golden brown, 3 to 4 minutes. Add the cabbage and cook, stirring, until wilted, about 5 minutes. Stir in the chicken broth, caraway seeds, bay leaves, salt, pepper, and thyme. Cook, uncovered, until the sauce comes to a boil. Add the pork chops, cover, reduce the heat to medium-low (180°F), and simmer until the pork chops are fork-tender, about 1½ hours. Remove the bay leaves.

Serve the pork chops with the cabbage and pan juices.

4 large pork chops (about 2 pounds)

2 teaspoons Cajun seasoning

¼ cup all-purpose flour

2 tablespoons olive oil

2 Granny Smith apples, peeled, cored, and cut into thick wedges

1 large onion, thinly sliced (about 2 cups)

1 head cabbage (about 3 pounds), chopped

2 cups chicken broth

½ teaspoon caraway seeds

2 bay leaves

2 teaspoons salt

1 teaspoon freshly ground black pepper

½ teaspoon dried thyme

SKILLET CHICKEN
with Cherry-Jalapeño Sauce

STRIKING A BALANCE BETWEEN SWEET AND SPICY NOTES, this simple dish is a nice alternative to barbecue and an easy way to dress up plain chicken breasts. The recipe works well with frozen cherries, so it's a good backup pantry dish you can put together on the fly. If you don't have jalapeños handy, use ½ teaspoon cayenne or ground chipotle instead.

CHICKEN

4 boneless, skinless chicken breasts (about 2 pounds)

Salt and freshly ground black pepper

¼ cup all-purpose flour

1 tablespoon olive oil

CHERRY-JALAPEÑO SAUCE

1 large shallot, thinly sliced

1 large jalapeño, seeded and finely chopped

1 large clove garlic, minced

1 cup frozen cherries

¼ cup dried cherries

¼ cup chicken broth

2 tablespoons brown sugar

1 tablespoon unsalted butter

TO MAKE THE CHICKEN: Season the chicken generously with salt and pepper. Lightly dredge in the flour.

In a large ferrous-bottomed skillet over medium-high heat (360°F), warm the olive oil. Cook the chicken, turning halfway through the cooking time, until golden brown and crispy, 15 to 18 minutes. Transfer the chicken to a plate and cover to keep warm.

TO MAKE THE CHERRY-JALAPEÑO SAUCE: In the same skillet, add the shallot, jalapeño, and garlic. Cook, stirring occasionally, until the vegetables soften, 2 to 3 minutes. Add the frozen cherries, dried cherries, chicken broth, and brown sugar, scraping the skillet with a wooden spoon to loosen any darkened bits that have accumulated on the bottom. Reduce the heat to low (180°F) and simmer for 10 minutes, until the sauce begins to thicken. Add the butter and return the chicken and any accumulated juices to the skillet to cook, covered, until a thermometer inserted into the thickest part registers 165°F. Serve the chicken topped with the cherry-jalapeño sauce.

Pecan-Crusted
CHICKEN BREASTS

SERVES
4

THIS IS THE RECIPE TO TRY WHEN YOU WANT a healthier alternative to traditional fried chicken. And because it's all too easy to burn the nuts in a dish like this, your induction burner comes to the rescue! Precise control makes it easy to quickly reduce the heat a few degrees and avoid that scenario completely.

In a shallow bowl, combine the pecans, flour, and salt.

In a small bowl, combine the syrup and mustard. Brush the chicken breasts with the syrup-mustard mixture. Coat the chicken breasts completely with the nut mixture, pressing firmly to ensure the coating sticks to the chicken.

In a large ferrous-bottomed skillet over medium-high heat (300°F), melt the butter and stir in the olive oil. Add the chicken, and cook for 15 to 18 minutes, turning halfway through the cooking time, until the chicken is browned on all sides and a thermometer inserted into the thickest part registers 165°F.

1 cup finely chopped pecans

¼ cup all-purpose flour

1 teaspoon salt

2 tablespoons maple syrup

1 tablespoon Dijon mustard

4 boneless skinless chicken breasts
(about 2 pounds)

2 tablespoons unsalted butter

1 tablespoon olive oil

Lemon
CHICKEN PICCATA

THIS BRIGHTLY FLAVORED DISH IS A SNAP TO PREPARE on an induction cooktop. If thin cutlets aren't available at your grocery, butterfly two boneless, skinless breasts yourself. Simply put your chicken breast on a cutting board and place your hand flat on top of it to hold it steady; using a sharp knife held parallel to the board, carefully slice into one side of the breast, starting at the thicker end and ending at the thin point, to yield two cutlets.

4 boneless, skinless chicken breast cutlets (about 1 pound)

Salt and freshly ground black pepper

¼ cup all-purpose flour

4 tablespoons unsalted butter, divided

4 tablespoons olive oil, divided

Zest and juice of 2 lemons

½ cup chicken broth

¼ cup brined capers, rinsed

2 tablespoons chopped
fresh parsley

Use a paper towel to pat the chicken dry. Season generously with salt and pepper, and then dredge the chicken in the flour.

In a large ferrous-bottomed skillet over medium-high heat (360°F), melt 1 tablespoon of the butter with 2 tablespoons of the olive oil. When the butter and oil start to sizzle, add 2 pieces of chicken and cook for 3 minutes per side, until browned. Remove and transfer to a plate. Melt 1 more tablespoon of the butter and add the remaining 2 tablespoons olive oil. When the butter and oil start to sizzle, add the remaining 2 pieces of chicken and brown both sides in the same manner. Remove the chicken to the plate and cover lightly to keep warm.

Into the same skillet, add the lemon zest and juice, broth, and capers. Bring to a boil, scraping up any brown bits from the skillet for extra flavor. Reduce the heat to medium-low (180°F). Return the chicken to the skillet along with any accumulated juices and simmer for 5 minutes. Remove the chicken to a platter. Add the remaining 2 tablespoons butter to the sauce and whisk vigorously. Pour the sauce over the chicken and sprinkle with the parsley before serving.

PAN-SEARED CHICKEN BREASTS
with Creamy Mustard Sauce

SERVES
4

IN LESS THAN 20 MINUTES, THIS FLAVORFUL CHICKEN can be on your dinner table! Have a cast-iron skillet? See what it can do beyond cooking—use it to flatten chicken breasts and other cuts of meat so it cooks more quickly and evenly, like in this recipe.

4 boneless, skinless chicken breasts (about 2 pounds)

Salt and freshly ground black pepper

3 tablespoons unsalted butter

1 shallot, finely chopped

¼ teaspoon dried thyme

⅓ cup dry white wine

⅓ cup chicken broth

⅓ cup heavy cream

2 tablespoons Dijon mustard

Use a paper towel to pat the chicken dry. Working one at a time, place a chicken breast between 2 sheets of parchment paper. Using a meat pounder or the flat bottom of a heavy pan, lightly pound the chicken until it is about ½ inch thick. Season the chicken generously with salt and pepper.

In a large ferrous-bottomed skillet over medium-high heat (360°F), melt the butter. Add the shallot and thyme and cook until the shallot softens, 1 to 2 minutes. Add the chicken breasts and cook, turning once, until golden on both sides and a thermometer inserted into the thickest part registers 165°F, 8 to 10 minutes total. Transfer the chicken to a plate and cover lightly to keep warm.

In the same skillet, add the wine and chicken broth. Bring to a boil, scraping up any brown bits from the skillet for extra flavor. Boil until the liquid is reduced by half, 1 to 2 minutes. Reduce the heat to medium (240°F) and stir in the cream and mustard. Cook for 1 minute to blend the flavors. Reduce the heat to medium-low (180°F). Return all the chicken to the skillet along with any accumulated juices and simmer for 2 minutes.

Home-Style
CHICKEN &
DUMPLINGS

WIDELY REGARDED AS THE ULTIMATE COMFORT FOOD, this is the sort of dish that's ideal for induction because you use your Dutch oven first to brown your chicken, imparting extra flavor in the finished dish, and then as a slow cooker. And best of all, you don't have any extra pots to clean!

Sprinkle the chicken with salt and pepper. Heat the oil in a large ferrous-bottomed Dutch oven over medium-high heat (360°F). Brown the chicken in batches, 4 to 6 minutes per side. Transfer to a plate.

Into the same pot, add the celery and carrots, and cook, stirring, until the vegetables begin to soften, 5 to 7 minutes. Add the chicken, onion halves, bay leaf, and water. Bring to a simmer, then reduce the heat to medium (240°F) and cook until the chicken is fork-tender, 25 to 30 minutes. Discard the onion and bay leaf and transfer the chicken to a plate; when cool enough to handle, use 2 forks to shred the chicken and then return it to the pot (discarding the skin and bones).

In a small bowl, whisk together ½ cup of the flour, 2 cups of the cooking liquid, and ¼ teaspoon each salt and pepper. Slowly whisk the flour mixture back into the pot. Simmer, stirring occasionally, until slightly thickened, 8 to 10 minutes.

In a medium bowl, whisk together the remaining 2 cups flour, baking powder, baking soda, and remaining ¼ teaspoon each salt and pepper. Whisk in the butter and buttermilk. Reduce the heat to medium-low (180°F) and drop the mixture into the broth in 6 large spoonfuls. Simmer, covered, until the dumplings firm, 12 to 15 minutes.

Return the chicken to the pot and simmer for 2 to 3 minutes, until heated through.

6 bone-in chicken thighs
(about 2½ pounds)

½ teaspoon salt, divided,
plus more for sprinkling

½ teaspoon freshly ground
black pepper, divided, plus more
for sprinkling

1 tablespoon olive oil

2 ribs celery, chopped

2 carrots, peeled and chopped

1 onion, halved

1 bay leaf

10 cups water

2½ cups all-purpose flour, divided

1 tablespoon baking powder

½ teaspoon baking soda

6 tablespoons unsalted butter, melted

¾ cup buttermilk

Simple CHICKEN CACCIATORE

SERVES
6

BRAISED IN A TOMATO-WINE SAUCE and accompanied by a variety of tender vegetables, this chicken dish is best served with your favorite starchy side—cheesy polenta, garlicky mashed potatoes, and a simple pasta dressed with olive oil are all good choices. If you prefer both light and dark chicken, cut a whole 4-pound chicken into six pieces to use in place of the thighs.

8 bone-in, skin-on chicken thighs
(about 4 pounds)

Salt

2 tablespoons olive oil

1 onion, halved and sliced

1 red or green bell pepper, cored,
seeded, and coarsely chopped

4 cloves garlic, thinly sliced

⅓ cup dry white or red wine

1 can (28 ounces) plum tomatoes in
their juice, preferably San Marzano

1 teaspoon dried thyme, plus
fresh thyme for garnish (optional)

1 teaspoon dried oregano, plus
fresh oregano for garnish (optional)

½ teaspoon freshly ground
black pepper

Season the chicken generously on all sides with salt. In a large ferrous-bottomed Dutch oven over medium heat (270°F), heat the olive oil. Working in batches to avoid crowding the pan, cook the chicken, skin-side down, until nicely browned, about 5 minutes on each side. Transfer to a bowl and set aside. Drain off all but 2 tablespoons of the rendered fat.

Increase the heat to medium-high (360°F) and add the onion and bell pepper. Cook, stirring frequently, until the onion is translucent, about 10 minutes. Add the garlic and cook for 1 minute.

Add the wine and bring to boil, scraping up any brown bits from the pot for extra flavor, until the liquid is reduced by half, 1 to 2 minutes. Add the tomatoes, thyme, oregano, pepper, and about 1 teaspoon salt. Reduce the heat to medium-low (180°F). Taste and adjust the seasonings as necessary. Arrange the chicken pieces on top of the tomatoes and onions, skin-side up. Cook, covered with the lid slightly ajar, until the thighs are very tender, 30 to 40 minutes. Top with fresh thyme and oregano if desired.

Apricot-Chicken
TAGINE

TAGINE, A TRADITIONAL MOROCCAN DISH SWEETENED with apricots and infused with rich, spicy flavors, makes a memorable meal to share with guests. It's especially delicious served with couscous, a type of small, rice-like pasta.

½ cup Turkish apricots

2 tablespoons honey

1 stick cinnamon

1½ cups water, divided

¼ cup sliced almonds

1 teaspoon ground cinnamon

1 teaspoon ground ginger

½ teaspoon ground turmeric

8 skinless, bone-in chicken thighs (about 2½ pounds)

Salt and freshly ground black pepper

2 tablespoons olive oil

1 tablespoon unsalted butter

1 large onion, chopped

4 cloves garlic, chopped

4 cups cooked couscous

In a small ferrous-bottomed saucepan over medium-high (300°F) heat, bring the apricots, honey, cinnamon stick, and 1 cup of the water to a boil. Reduce the heat to medium-low (180°F) and simmer, uncovered, until the apricots are very tender (add more water if necessary). Once the apricots are tender, simmer until the liquid is reduced to a glaze, 10 to 15 minutes. Discard the cinnamon stick and set the apricots aside.

In a small ferrous-bottomed skillet over medium-high heat (360°F), toast the almonds, stirring frequently, until toasted and fragrant, 3 to 5 minutes. Set the nuts aside.

In a small bowl, combine the cinnamon, ginger, and turmeric. Season the chicken generously with salt and pepper and sprinkle with the spice mixture to coat. In a ferrous-bottomed Dutch oven over medium-high heat (360°F), heat the olive oil and butter. Cook the chicken in batches, turning once, until browned, 8 to 12 minutes. Transfer to a plate.

In the same pot, add the onion and cook, stirring occasionally, until very soft, about 8 minutes. Add the garlic and cook until fragrant, about 1 minute longer. Return the chicken to the pot along with any accumulated juices. Add the remaining ½ cup water and reduce the heat to medium-low (180°F). Cover and simmer for 20 minutes, until the chicken is tender. Stir in the apricots and their cooking liquid. Cook, covered, for 10 minutes longer. Serve over the couscous topped with the reserved almonds.

Orange
CHICKEN STIR-FRY

SERVES
4

WHO NEEDS TAKEOUT WHEN YOU CAN WHIP UP orange chicken on your induction cooktop? For best results, use a pot and a wok to make the sauce and stir-fry separately. If you use just a wok, make the chicken and broccoli, transfer to a bowl, then rinse the wok and make the sauce before combining.

TO START THE STIR-FRY: In a shallow, medium bowl, toss the chicken pieces with the soy sauce and wine. Let stand while you make the sauce.

TO MAKE THE ORANGE SAUCE: Use a vegetable peeler to remove long strips of zest from each orange. Arrange the zest between paper towels and microwave on high in 20-second increments until dry but not browned, 60 to 80 seconds. When cool, finely chop and set aside.

In a small bowl, whisk together the juice and the 1 tablespoon cornstarch until the cornstarch is dissolved. Squeeze the juice from the oranges and add to the mixture.

In a medium ferrous-bottomed pot, heat the 1 tablespoon oil over medium heat (270°F). Add the garlic, ginger, red pepper flakes, and dried orange zest and stir-fry until golden, about 30 seconds. Add the soy sauce, wine, vinegar, and sugar and stir until the sugar dissolves, about 5 seconds. Stir the orange juice–cornstarch mixture, then add it to the skillet. Bring the sauce to a boil, stirring, then reduce the heat to medium-low (180°F) and simmer, uncovered, for 1 minute, until sauce begins to thicken. Set aside.

TO FINISH THE STIR-FRY: Put the ½ cup cornstarch in a large resealable plastic bag. Add the chicken pieces and shake vigorously to coat. Heat the ½ cup oil in a large wok over medium-high heat (360°F). Add the chicken and cook, stirring regularly, until the chicken is browned, about 5 minutes. Transfer the chicken to a plate. Add the broccoli and water. Cook, covered, until the broccoli is bright green and tender, 3 to 5 minutes. Return the chicken to the wok and toss with the sauce. Scatter the scallions on top just before serving with the rice.

STIR-FRY

2 boneless, skinless chicken breasts (about 1 pound), cut into 1½-inch pieces

1 teaspoon reduced-sodium soy sauce

1 teaspoon Chinese rice wine or dry sherry

½ cup cornstarch

½ cup canola oil

4 cups broccoli florets

2 tablespoons water

4 scallions, thinly sliced

4 cups cooked rice

ORANGE SAUCE

2 navel oranges

½ cup orange juice

1 tablespoon cornstarch

1 tablespoon canola oil

4 cloves garlic, minced

1 tablespoon grated fresh ginger

¼ teaspoon red pepper flakes

2 tablespoons reduced-sodium soy sauce

2 teaspoons Chinese rice wine or dry sherry

2 teaspoons cider vinegar

3 tablespoons sugar

Festive
CHICKEN FAJITAS

YOU CAN ADD SO MANY GOOD TOPPINGS to a fajita spread—guacamole, tortilla chips, sour cream, beans, and rice. But at the center of it all is a sizzling pile of peppers and chicken. Start this dish about 4 hours before you plan to serve it, so your chicken has plenty of time to marinate.

¼ cup vegetable oil, divided

Juice of 1 lemon

1 teaspoon salt

1 teaspoon dried oregano

1 teaspoon ground cumin

1 teaspoon garlic powder

½ teaspoon chili powder

½ teaspoon smoked paprika
 or ground chipotle (optional)

1½ pounds chicken tenders,
 cut into strips

2 bell peppers, color of your choice,
 cored, seeded, and sliced

1 red onion, sliced

¼ cup chopped scallions

½ cup salsa

8 flour tortillas, warmed

In a resealable plastic bag, combine 2 tablespoons of the oil, lemon juice, salt, oregano, cumin, garlic powder, chili powder, and paprika or chipotle (if using). Add the chicken and turn to coat. Refrigerate for at least 1 hour or up to 4 hours.

In a large ferrous-bottomed skillet over medium-high heat (360°F), heat 1 tablespoon of oil. Add the peppers and onion. Cook, stirring frequently, until the vegetables soften, about 5 minutes. Transfer the vegetables to a plate.

Add the remaining 1 tablespoon oil to the skillet. Add the chicken (discard the marinade) and cook, stirring frequently, until cooked through, about 5 minutes. Add the reserved vegetables to the skillet and cook until heated through, about 1 minute longer. Sprinkle the scallions on top and serve with the salsa and tortillas.

SKILLET ENCHILADAS
with Creamy Queso Sauce

CONTRARY TO TRADITION, ENCHILADAS DON'T HAVE TO BE BAKED for diners to enjoy their rich, satisfying flavors, and this recipe proves that point well. It's an excellent dish to make when you have leftover chicken or turkey breast.

¼ cup unsalted butter

¼ all-purpose flour

2 cups chicken broth

8 ounces sour cream

2 cups shredded pepper Jack cheese, divided

1 can (4.5 ounces) chopped green chiles

½ teaspoon cayenne pepper

3 cups chopped cooked chicken breast

1 small onion, finely chopped

8 flour tortillas

1 can (2.25 ounces) sliced black olives, drained

In a large ferrous-bottomed skillet over medium-high heat (300°F), melt the butter. Add the flour and cook, stirring occasionally, until the flour begins to brown. Stir in the chicken broth and cook, stirring, until the mixture is smooth and bubbly. Add the sour cream, ½ cup of the cheese, chiles, and cayenne and stir until thoroughly combined. Turn off the cooktop.

In a large bowl, combine the chicken, onion, ¾ cup of the sauce, and ½ cup of cheese. Mix until thoroughly combined.

Reserve ¾ cup of the sauce (leave the rest in the skillet). To assemble the dish, fill each tortilla with ⅓ cup of the chicken mixture, then roll up and place seam-side down in the skillet. Pour the reserved sauce over the top of the tortillas. Cover and cook over medium heat (270°F) until heated through, about 20 minutes. Top with the remaining 1 cup cheese and the olives. Cover and let sit until the cheese is melted, about 5 minutes.

Super-Easy
TURKEY MEATLOAF

YOU CAN EVEN USE YOUR INDUCTION COOKTOP to make the family favorite, meatloaf! Each diner gets an individual loaf. The secret to success is first searing the loaves to develop a nice crust and then steaming them over low heat, which also guarantees exceptionally moist and delicious results.

Combine the bread and milk in a large bowl and let sit for 5 minutes. Add the egg, Worcestershire sauce, onion, celery, paprika, salt, and pepper. Whisk with a fork until thoroughly combined. Add the turkey and mix with your clean hands until combined. Shape into six 3- to 4-inch oval loaves.

In a large ferrous-bottomed nonstick skillet over medium-high heat (360°F), heat the olive oil. Add the loaves and brown for about 3 minutes per side.

Whisk the ketchup, sugar, and vinegar in a bowl and brush a few tablespoonfuls of the mixture over the meat. Add the water to the skillet, cover, and reduce the heat to medium-low (180°F). Simmer until cooked through and a thermometer inserted into the thickest part of a loaf registers 165°F, about 15 minutes.

Transfer the loaves to a plate. Add the remaining ketchup mixture to the skillet and cook over high heat, stirring, until thick, 3 to 5 minutes. Serve the meatloaves with the hot glaze drizzled on top and sprinkled with the parsley.

1 slice bread, torn into small pieces

⅓ cup milk

1 egg

3 tablespoons Worcestershire sauce

1 small onion, finely chopped

1 rib celery, finely chopped

1 teaspoon paprika

1 teaspoon salt

½ teaspoon freshly ground black pepper

1½ pounds lean ground turkey

1 tablespoon olive oil

½ cup ketchup

2 tablespoons brown sugar

1 tablespoon cider vinegar

½ cup water

2 tablespoons chopped fresh parsley

Skillet
TURKEY TETRAZZINI

SERVES
4

YOU CAN TRANSFORM LEFTOVER TURKEY BREAST into a fabulous one-dish meal your family will love with the help of your induction cooktop! If you don't have turkey on hand, rotisserie chicken makes a fine substitute.

2 teaspoons olive oil

1 small onion, chopped

8 ounces brown mushrooms, chopped

1 clove garlic, minced

½ teaspoon dried thyme

4 cups milk

4 cups reduced-sodium chicken broth

1 pound cavatappi pasta

½ cup cream cheese

¾ cup grated Parmesan

1 cup frozen peas

2 cups cooked, chopped turkey breast

In a large, deep ferrous-bottomed skillet, heat the olive oil over medium-high heat (360°F). Add the onion and cook until tender, 3 to 4 minutes. Add the mushrooms, garlic, and thyme, and continue cooking until the mushrooms soften, 3 to 5 minutes. Transfer the vegetables to a bowl and set aside.

To the same skillet, add the milk and broth and raise the heat to high (450°F). Bring to a boil and stir in the pasta. Cook the pasta, stirring often to prevent scorching, until just tender, 5 to 7 minutes. Reduce the heat to medium-low (180°F) and stir in the cream cheese and Parmesan. Cook, stirring occasionally, until the mixture thickens, 5 to 8 minutes. Stir in the reserved mushroom mixture, peas, and turkey. Cook, stirring occasionally, until warmed through, about another 2 minutes.

Turkey PICADILLO

PICADILLO IS A CUBAN DISH TRADITIONALLY MADE with ground beef, but lean ground turkey works just as well and makes it a bit healthier. The olives and raisins play off one another nicely. A bonus: This dish comes together in less than 30 minutes!

Heat the olive oil in a large, ferrous-bottomed skillet over medium-high heat (360°F). Cook the turkey until evenly browned, breaking up the meat with the side of a spoon as it cooks, 8 to 10 minutes. Add the onion, bell pepper, garlic, cumin, and cayenne and cook until the onion has softened, about 5 minutes. Stir in the bay leaf, wine, tomato sauce, olives, and raisins. Reduce the heat to medium-low (180°F) and simmer, covered, stirring occasionally, until the raisins are plump and tender, about 15 minutes. Remove the bay leaf, sprinkle the parsley on top, and serve over brown rice.

1 tablespoon olive oil

1 pound lean ground turkey

1 large onion, chopped

1 green or red bell pepper, cored, seeded, and chopped

4 cloves garlic, minced

2 teaspoons ground cumin

1 teaspoon cayenne pepper

1 bay leaf

½ cup dry red wine

1 can (8 ounces) tomato sauce

½ cup chopped green olives

½ cup raisins

2 tablespoons chopped fresh parsley

3 cups cooked brown rice

SEARED SCALLOPS
with Spicy Orange Sauce

LARGE SEA SCALLOPS ARE ANOTHER DISH that many people only enjoy in a restaurant because they consider them too difficult to cook at home. This recipe, however, will show you how simple it really is to prepare them well. Here they are dressed in a rich orange sauce instead of the traditional lemon-and-butter combination, and this impressive topping also works nicely over grilled chicken or salmon.

ORANGE SAUCE

2 tablespoons sugar

Juice of 3 medium oranges
plus 1 tablespoon zest

Juice of 1 lemon

1 tablespoon apple cider vinegar

½ teaspoon ground coriander

Pinch of cayenne pepper

3 tablespoons unsalted butter,
divided

SCALLOPS

1½ pounds large, dry sea scallops

Salt and freshly ground black pepper

1 tablespoon olive oil

2 tablespoons chopped fresh cilantro

TO MAKE THE ORANGE SAUCE: In a small ferrous-bottomed pot over medium-high heat (330°F), cook the sugar, stirring occasionally, until the sugar liquifies and begins to darken, 2 to 3 minutes. Remove from the cooktop and whisk in the citrus juices, zest, vinegar, coriander, and cayenne.

Return the pot to the cooktop and boil until thick, stirring often, about 5 minutes. Remove the pot from the cooktop, place on a heatproof surface, and whisk in 2 tablespoons of the butter. Cover and set aside.

TO MAKE THE SCALLOPS: Use paper towels to blot the sea scallops dry. Season generously with salt and pepper. Heat the oil and remaining tablespoon of butter in a large ferrous-bottomed skillet over high heat (390°F). Add the scallops, flat-side down with ample space between them, and sear until golden, 1½ to 2 minutes. Flip and cook until golden on the other side, 1½ to 2 minutes. Drizzle the orange sauce over the scallops and top with the cilantro.

COD *Niçoise*

TOMATOES, OLIVES, ARTICHOKES, AND CAPERS are the perfect accompaniment to light, flaky cod. Serve with French bread, a light garden salad, and a crisp Chardonnay for a restaurant-quality meal.

2 cups cherry tomatoes, halved

¾ cup coarsely chopped, pitted Kalamata olives

¾ cup canned artichoke hearts, quartered

2 tablespoons capers, drained

4 (6-ounce) cod fillets

Salt and freshly cracked black pepper

½ teaspoon herbes de Provence

3 tablespoons olive oil, divided

¼ cup finely chopped red onion

1 lemon, halved, plus more for serving

¼ cup chopped fresh parsley

In a medium bowl, combine the tomatoes, olives, artichokes, and capers. Pat the fish dry and season generously with salt, pepper, and the herbes de Provence. Set aside.

In a large, ferrous-bottomed nonstick skillet over medium-high heat (360°F), warm 1 tablespoon of the oil. Arrange the fish fillets in the skillet and reduce the heat to medium (240°F). Cook, turning once, until the fish flakes easily with a fork, 3 to 5 minutes. Transfer the fish to a serving plate.

Remove the skillet to a heatproof surface. Using tongs, carefully wipe out the skillet with a paper towel. Return the skillet to the cooking surface. Add another 1 tablespoon of oil and the onion. Cook, shaking the skillet for about 30 seconds, then add the tomato mixture. Cook for another 30 seconds. Juice the lemon into the skillet. Add the parsley and stir to coat. Cook for another 30 seconds, or until the tomatoes begin to soften. Remove the skillet from the heat, spoon the sauce over the fish, and serve with more lemon on the side.

Cajun
CATFISH

SERVES
6

THE DOWN-HOME FLAVOR OF THESE CRISPY FISH nuggets is irresistible! To make your own tartar sauce, combine 1½ cups mayonnaise, ½ cup pickle relish, 3 tablespoons vinegar, 3 tablespoons drained capers, and 1 tablespoon Dijon mustard. Season to taste with salt and pepper.

In a resealable plastic bag, combine the fish and buttermilk. Refrigerate for 30 minutes to 1 hour.

Meanwhile, in another resealable bag, combine the flour, cornmeal, Cajun seasoning, onion powder, garlic powder, and cayenne (if using). In a small, shallow bowl, combine the juice from ½ lemon and the egg. Whisk until thoroughly combined. Chop the remaining lemon into wedges. Set aside.

In heavy, ferrous-bottomed 3-quart saucepan, heat the oil over medium-high heat (360°F) until a thermometer registers 360°F. Line a plate with paper towels.

Working with 5 to 6 pieces at a time, remove the catfish from the buttermilk mixture, dip it in the egg, and then transfer to the bag with the seasoning mix. Seal and shake gently to coat, then carefully slip the nuggets into the hot oil. Cook for 2 minutes, until lightly browned. Use a slotted spoon to turn the pieces over and fry until cooked through, another minute or two. Transfer the fish to the prepared plate and repeat with the remaining ingredients. Serve warm with the reserved lemon wedges and tartar sauce on the side.

2 pounds catfish fillets, cut into 2-inch pieces

1 cup buttermilk

¾ cup all-purpose flour

¾ cup stone-ground cornmeal

2 tablespoons Cajun Creole seasoning

1 teaspoon onion powder

1 teaspoon garlic powder

½ teaspoon cayenne pepper (optional)

1 lemon, halved

1 egg, lightly beaten

2 cups vegetable oil

1½ cups tartar sauce (see headnote)

Perfectly
POACHED SALMON

YOU'RE PRACTICALLY GUARANTEED PERFECT RESULTS if you start your salmon in cold water. Serve the cooked salmon warm or cold topped with your favorite sauce—though it's quite delicious served simply plain as well.

4 cups cold water

2 ribs celery, coarsely chopped

1 onion, halved

Juice of 1 lemon

1½ teaspoons salt

½ teaspoon peppercorns

1 bay leaf

1½ pounds salmon fillet

In a large, ferrous-bottomed saucepan, combine the water, celery, onion, lemon juice, salt, peppercorns, and bay leaf. Add the salmon and additional water, if necessary, to ensure the fish is completely covered. Set over medium heat (240°F) and bring to a very gentle simmer (adjust the heat if the water begins to boil). Cook until the fish is opaque and cooked through, about 20 minutes, or until a thermometer registers 115°F when inserted into the thickest part of the fish. (Cooking time may vary based on the thickness of the fish, so check the temperature to determine doneness.) Carefully transfer the salmon to a plate to rest for 5 minutes before serving.

Honey-Glazed
SALMON

SERVES
4

SALMON MATCHES WELL TO THE SPICY SWEETNESS of this easy-to-assemble glaze. Once you have the technique down, try this same method with your favorite barbecue or honey-mustard sauce.

In a small bowl, whisk together the honey, soy sauce, juice from 1 lemon, and red pepper flakes; set aside. Season the salmon generously with salt and pepper.

In a large ferrous-bottomed nonstick skillet over medium-high heat (300°F), heat 1 tablespoon of the oil. Add the salmon skin-side up and cook until deeply golden, about 6 minutes, then flip over and add the remaining 1 tablespoon oil.

Slice the remaining lemon and add to the skillet along with the honey mixture. Cook, basting the fish occasionally, until the sauce is reduced and begins to thicken, about 2 minutes longer. Garnish with the sliced lemon and serve.

¼ cup honey

¼ cup reduced-sodium soy sauce

2 lemons, divided

½ teaspoon red pepper flakes

4 (6-ounce) salmon fillets

Salt and freshly ground black pepper

2 tablespoons olive oil, divided

SHRIMP SCAMPI
with Asparagus & Tomatoes

HERE'S ANOTHER DELICIOUS RECIPE THAT PROVES how easy it is to cook several parts of a meal with one cooktop. For best results, make sure you have all your ingredients prepped and measured before you begin.

Fill a ferrous-bottomed soup pot with water, add 1 teaspoon of salt, and bring to a rolling boil over high heat (450°F). Add the pasta and stir gently to ensure the noodles are completely covered. When the water begins to boil again, remove the pot from the heat and set on a heatproof surface. Cover and let sit according to the time indicated on the package directions (usually 8 to 10 minutes), then drain.

Meanwhile, in a large ferrous-bottomed skillet, heat 1 tablespoon of the olive oil over medium-high heat (360°F). Add the asparagus and 2 tablespoons of water. Season with a generous pinch of salt. Cover and cook until the asparagus is tender, 3 to 5 minutes. Transfer the asparagus to a plate and return the skillet to the cooktop.

Warm the remaining 1 tablespoon oil. Add the garlic and red pepper flakes (if using). Cook until fragrant, about 30 seconds. Add the shrimp, season with salt and pepper, and cook until they have turned pink, 2 to 3 minutes. Remove the shrimp from the skillet; set aside and keep warm. Add the tomatoes, wine, and lemon juice and bring to a boil. Add the butter. When the butter has melted and the tomatoes begin to soften, return the shrimp to the skillet along with the asparagus, parsley, and cooked pasta. Toss well to coat and adjust the seasoning if necessary before serving.

1 pound linguine

Salt and freshly ground black pepper

2 tablespoons olive oil, divided

1 pound asparagus, trimmed and chopped into 2-inch pieces

4 cloves garlic, minced

½ teaspoon red pepper flakes (optional)

1 pound large shrimp, peeled and deveined

1 cup halved cherry tomatoes

½ cup dry white wine

Juice of 1 lemon

2 tablespoons unsalted butter

2 tablespoons chopped fresh parsley

GREEK SHRIMP
with Lemony Orzo

QUICK-COOKING SHRIMP AND ORZO, a rice-shaped pasta, make this one-pot meal a cinch to put together—in less than 20 minutes! Round out the time-saving dinner with a simple green salad and pita bread.

2 tablespoons olive oil

6 cloves garlic, minced

1 pint grape tomatoes, halved

1 teaspoon salt

1 teaspoon dried oregano

12 ounces orzo

3½ cups reduced-sodium chicken broth

1 pound large shrimp, peeled and deveined

½ cup Kalamata olives, coarsely chopped

Juice of 1 lemon

4 ounces feta, crumbled

2 tablespoons chopped fresh parsley

In a large nonstick, ferrous-bottomed skilled, warm the olive oil over medium-high heat (360°F). Add the garlic, tomatoes, salt, and oregano and cook until the garlic is fragrant, about 30 seconds. Add the orzo and stir until evenly coated. Add the broth and reduce the heat to medium-low (180°F). Simmer, covered, for 10 minutes, until most of the liquid is absorbed. Stir in the shrimp, olives, and lemon juice. Cover and continue cooking for another 5 minutes, until the shrimp are pink and cooked through. Top with the feta and parsley just before serving.

Creamy
SHRIMP & GRITS

SERVES
4

NO LONGER JUST A LOW COUNTRY FISHERMAN'S BREAKFAST, this delicious dish can now be found in fine dining restaurants. However, you can make your own version relatively easily with your induction cooktop.

In a medium ferrous-bottomed pot, bring 3 cups of the water to a boil over high heat (450°F). Add the salt. Fill a large liquid measuring cup with the remaining 1½ cups cold water, then whisk in the grits until smooth. When the pot of water begins to boil, add the grits and water mixture, stirring constantly with a wooden spoon to avoid lumps from forming. When all the grits are incorporated, and the water has begun to boil again, reduce the heat to medium-low (180°F) and simmer, stirring occasionally, until thick, 30 to 35 minutes. Remove from the heat, stir in the butter and cheese, and let sit, covered, while preparing the shrimp.

Place the bacon in a large, heavy ferrous-bottomed skillet and set over medium heat (240°F). Cook until crispy, 5 to 7 minutes. Transfer the bacon to a plate and reserve about 3 tablespoons of the pan drippings. Add the onion, bell pepper, and Cajun seasoning. Cook, stirring occasionally, until the vegetables soften, about 5 minutes. Increase the heat to medium-high (360°F). Add the shrimp, garlic, and reserved bacon and cook, stirring constantly, for 1 to 2 minutes. Stir in the chicken broth and cook, stirring occasionally, until the shrimp are cooked through, about 5 minutes. Stir in the lemon juice. Taste and adjust the seasonings. Serve the shrimp over the grits, topped with the scallions and parsley.

4½ cups cold water

1 teaspoon salt

1 cup stone-ground grits

2 tablespoons unsalted butter

1½ cups shredded
white Cheddar cheese

4 thick slices bacon, chopped

1 small white onion, chopped

½ green bell pepper, chopped

½ teaspoon Cajun seasoning

1½ pounds large shrimp,
peeled and deveined

4 cloves garlic, minced

1 cup chicken broth

Juice of 1 lemon

3 scallions, chopped

2 tablespoons chopped
fresh parsley

Crispy CALAMARI

DON'T WAIT TO DINE OUT TO ENJOY CALAMARI! It's easier than you may think to make it at home for a fraction of the cost. An induction burner is especially helpful for holding your oil at the right temperature, but be sure to watch the cooking time—overcooked calamari are tough and chewy. Fry up the tentacles, too, if you enjoy them, but keep in mind they'll need a few seconds longer cooking time.

2 cups buttermilk

1½ teaspoons salt, plus more
for sprinkling

4 cloves garlic, smashed

1 pound cleaned medium squid
(4 to 5 inches), sliced into ¼-inch rings

½ cup all-purpose flour

½ cup cornstarch

⅓ cup yellow cornmeal

½ teaspoon freshly ground
black pepper

2–3 cups peanut, canola,
or other vegetable oil

4 lemon wedges

1 cup marina sauce, warmed

In a resealable plastic bag, combine the buttermilk, ½ teaspoon of the salt, garlic, and squid. Seal, shake to coat, and refrigerate for 4 hours or preferably overnight.

In another resealable bag, combine the flour, cornstarch, cornmeal, 1 teaspoon of salt, and the pepper. Set aside. Line a baking sheet with paper towels.

Fill a deep, ferrous-bottomed pot with 2 to 3 cups of oil (no more than halfway full) and place over medium heat (360°F). Use a candy or deep-fry thermometer to adjust the cooktop as necessary to maintain a steady heat at 360°F. Working in batches, remove a handful of squid from the buttermilk, squeeze gently to remove excess buttermilk, and transfer to the bag with the flour mixture. Seal and shake the bag gently to coat. Carefully add the squid to the hot oil. Use tongs to loosen any pieces that stick to the bottom of the pot and turn gently as necessary to ensure even browning. Cook until lightly browned, about 1½ minutes. Use a slotted spot to remove the squid to the baking sheet. Repeat with remaining squid. Sprinkle with a generous pinch of salt and serve with the lemon wedges and marinara sauce for dipping.

SPAGHETTI
with Garlic Confit

HERE'S AN APPETIZING DISH YOU CAN THROW TOGETHER with items probably already in your pantry. To cook something "confit" requires a long, slow cooking time, so an induction cooktop is the ideal solution, especially when turning on your oven to roast a bit of garlic may seem like overkill.

1 head garlic, peeled and separated into cloves

1 large sprig rosemary (optional)

½ teaspoon red pepper flakes

1½ teaspoons salt, divided

½ cup olive oil

1 pound spaghetti

¼ cup grated Parmesan

¼ cup chopped fresh parsley

In a small ferrous-bottomed pot over medium-low heat (180°F), combine the garlic, rosemary (if using), pepper flakes, ½ teaspoon of the salt, and olive oil. Make sure the garlic is completely covered by the oil (add a little more if necessary). Reduce the heat to 150°F and simmer for 1 hour, until the garlic is very soft. Remove from the heat and let cool on a heatproof surface. Remove the rosemary sprig, if using.

Fill a ferrous-bottomed soup pot with water, add the remaining 1 teaspoon salt, and bring to a rolling boil over high heat (450°F). Add the pasta and stir gently to ensure the noodles are completely covered. When the water begins to boil again, remove the pot from the heat and set on a heatproof surface. Cover and let sit according to the time indicated on the package directions (usually 8 to 10 minutes).

Drain the pasta when it is "al dente." Toss with the garlic and oil mixture. Sprinkle the Parmesan and parsley on top just before serving.

Perfect
PAD THAI

**SERVES
4**

THIS CLASSIC STIR-FRY REQUIRES VERY LITTLE hands-on cooking time, making it a great choice for busy evenings. Tamarind paste, which is widely available in Asian groceries, stays good for years when refrigerated—keep some on hand for whipping up this easy, go-to dish.

Soak the noodles in a large bowl of warm water until softened, 25 to 30 minutes. Drain well in a colander and cover with a dampened paper towel.

Meanwhile, make the sauce by combining the tamarind paste and boiling-hot water in a small bowl, stirring occasionally, until softened, about 5 minutes. Add the soy sauce, brown sugar, and sriracha, stirring until the sugar has dissolved.

Heat 2 tablespoons of the oil in a large, ferrous-bottomed wok or skillet over medium-high heat (330°F). Fry the tofu, gently turning occasionally, until golden, 5 to 8 minutes. Transfer the tofu to a plate lined with paper towels. Add 1 tablespoon of the oil to the wok and lower the heat to medium (270°F). Cook the eggs, stirring gently with a spatula, until cooked through, about 1 minute. Transfer to a plate. Add the remaining 1 tablespoon oil to the wok and stir-fry the shallots, scallions, and garlic until the vegetables soften, about 1 minute. Add the drained noodles, tofu, bean sprouts, and sauce. Cook, tossing gently, until the noodles are tender, 3 to 5 minutes. Stir in the eggs and transfer to a large shallow serving dish. Sprinkle the peanuts and cilantro on top. Serve with the lime wedges and additional sriracha (if using).

12 ounces dried flat rice noodles

3 tablespoons tamarind paste

1 cup boiling-hot water

½ cup reduced-sodium soy sauce

¼ cup packed light brown sugar

2 tablespoons sriracha,
plus more for topping

4 tablespoons vegetable oil, divided

1 package (14 to 16 ounces) firm tofu,
pressed and cut into ½-inch cubes

4 large eggs, lightly beaten

2 shallots, sliced

1 bunch scallions, chopped

4 cloves garlic, minced

2 cups bean sprouts (about ¼ pound)

½ cup roasted peanuts,
coarsely chopped

½ cup chopped fresh cilantro

Lime wedges, for serving

Stovetop
MAC & CHEESE

FORGET ABOUT THE BOXED STUFF, and don't bother to turn on your oven! You can enjoy a delicious mac and cheese made easily with a few simple ingredients and your induction cooktop.

Fill a ferrous-bottomed pot with water and bring to a rolling boil over high heat (450°F). Add the pasta and stir gently to ensure the noodles are completely covered. When the water begins to boil again, remove the pot from the heat and set on a heatproof surface. Cover and let sit according to the time indicated on the package directions (usually 6 to 8 minutes), then drain.

Meanwhile, in another ferrous-bottomed pot over medium-high heat (300°F), melt the butter. Whisk in the flour, mustard, and salt. Cook the butter and flour mixture until it begins to brown, 3 to 5 minutes. Slowly whisk in the milk, stirring until smooth. Add the cheeses and cook, whisking frequently, until melted. Stir in the drained pasta and toss gently to coat. Serve with the hot sauce on the side (if using).

8 ounces elbow pasta

3 tablespoons unsalted butter

3 tablespoons all-purpose flour

1 teaspoon Dijon mustard

1 teaspoon salt

1¾ cups milk

1 bag (8 ounces) shredded sharp Cheddar cheese

4 ounces cream cheese, at room temperature and cubed

Hot sauce (optional)

Favorite
CHEESE FONDUE

SERVES
4

A GOOD FONDUE REQUIRES A GENTLE HEAT, making this an ideal dish to try with your induction cooktop. But be forewarned: You may want to kiss your old fondue pot and those smelly Sterno cans goodbye.

1 medium clove garlic, cut
in half

1 cup dry white wine,
plus more as needed

½ pound Emmentaler cheese, grated

½ pound Gruyère cheese, grated

1 tablespoon cornstarch

1 tablespoon fresh lemon juice

Kosher salt and freshly ground
black pepper

Toasted bread cubes and/or lightly
blanched vegetables, for dipping

Rub the cut faces of the garlic around the inside of a heavy, 1-quart ferrous-bottomed pot. Add the wine and warm over medium-low heat (180°F) until steaming. Meanwhile, place both cheeses and the cornstarch in a resealable plastic bag and toss until evenly coated.

Add the cheese mixture, 1 handful at a time, to the pot, stirring until mostly melted before adding the next handful. Continue until all the cheese is melted into the wine, forming a smooth, glossy melted cheese sauce, about 10 minutes. Stir in the lemon juice until fully incorporated. Season with salt and pepper. Reduce the heat to the lowest setting to keep warm (ideally 100°F to 110°F). Serve with the bread and vegetables for dipping. If the fondue begins to thicken too much, stir in a small splash of wine.

Curried CHICKPEAS & POTATOES

SERVES 6

DON'T LET INDIAN FOOD INTIMIDATE YOU in the kitchen. A longer list of ingredients doesn't necessarily mean more work. This recipe is a perfect example: it's all flavor, no fuss. And it's so hearty and satisfying that you'll forget that it's vegetarian!

In a ferrous-bottomed Dutch oven over medium-high heat (360°F), heat the oil. Add the onion, garlic, and ginger, and cook, stirring occasionally, until the onion is translucent, about for 3 minutes. Stir in the curry powder and cumin. Cook until fragrant, about 30 seconds. Add the potatoes, chickpeas, tomatoes, coconut milk, and vegetable broth. Bring to a boil, then reduce the heat to medium-low (180°F) and simmer, stirring occasionally, until the potatoes are tender and the sauce has thickened, about 25 minutes. Stir in the scallions, lime juice, and cilantro. Season to taste with salt. Top with additional cilantro, and serve with the rice.

3 tablespoons coconut or vegetable oil

1 large onion, chopped

2 large cloves garlic, minced

1 tablespoon grated fresh ginger

2 tablespoons curry powder

1 teaspoon ground cumin

2 large russet potatoes, cut into ½-inch cubes

2 cans (14 ounces) chickpeas, rinsed and drained

1 can (14 ounces) diced tomatoes

1 can (14 ounces) coconut milk

1 cup vegetable broth

2 scallions, chopped

Juice of 1 lime

2 tablespoons fresh cilantro plus more for garnish

Salt

6 cups cooked basmati rice

Mushroom RISOTTO

THIS RECIPE HELPS YOU GET PERFECT RISOTTO results without constant stirring. The secret is the slow, even heat your induction cooktop produces. Let it save you the work!

2 tablespoons olive oil

1½ pounds brown mushrooms, sliced

1 large shallot, chopped

1 teaspoon salt

2 tablespoons unsalted butter

1 cup Arborio rice

⅓ cup dry white wine

4 cups chicken broth

1 cup frozen peas

⅓ cup grated Parmesan

¼ cup chopped fresh parsley

Warm the olive oil in a large ferrous-bottomed skillet over medium-high heat (360°F). Add the mushrooms, and cook until soft, about 3 minutes. Add the shallot and cook until it begins to soften, about 1 minute longer. Add the salt and butter to the skillet. When the butter has melted, add the rice and stir until evenly coated, about 2 minutes. When the rice has taken on a pale, golden color, add the wine, stirring constantly until the wine is fully absorbed. Reduce the heat to medium (240°F). Add the broth to the rice, ½ cup at a time, stirring occasionally until the broth is absorbed. Continue adding the broth ½ cup at a time, stirring after each addition until the liquid is absorbed. Cook until the rice is al dente, 15 to 20 minutes.

Meanwhile, thaw the peas by placing them in a colander and running under warm water for 1 minute. Drain well.

Remove the skillet from heat and stir in the peas and Parmesan. Taste and adjust the seasonings if necessary. Sprinkle the parsley on top just before serving.

FRIED POLENTA
with Corn-Tomato Relish

A SUPER-EASY RELISH PAIRED WITH PREPARED POLENTA comes to the rescue for a weeknight meal. Look for prepared polenta in the refrigerated section of your grocer's produce department.

½ red onion, chopped

4 tablespoons olive oil, divided

2 teaspoons red wine vinegar

1½ cups grape tomatoes, halved

1 can (14 ounces) vacuum-packed corn, drained

¼ cup chopped fresh basil

½ teaspoon salt

2 tablespoons unsalted butter, divided

2 tubes (18 ounces) plain prepared polenta, sliced into 1-inch pieces

In a large bowl, combine the onion, 2 tablespoons of the olive oil, vinegar, tomatoes, corn, basil, and salt. Mix until thoroughly combined. Set aside.

In a large nonstick, ferrous-bottomed skillet over medium-high heat (360°F), heat 1 tablespoon of olive oil and 1 tablespoon of the butter. When the butter is melted, arrange half the polenta slices in the skillet and cook, turning once, until golden brown on both sides, about 10 minutes. Repeat with the remaining ingredients. Serve the polenta topped with the corn relish.

Cuban
BLACK BEANS & RICE

SERVES
6

YOU DON'T NEED TO SOAK YOUR BEANS. Letting them simmer on your induction cooktop along with some nice aromatics is all you need to guarantee perfect results.

In a ferrous-bottomed Dutch oven, combine the beans, onion, garlic, and bay leaf. Squeeze the juice from the orange and add it to the pot along with the spent halves. Add enough water to cover the beans by 3 to 4 inches. Cover and place over high heat (450°F) until the water comes to a boil, then reduce the heat to medium-low (180°F) and simmer, uncovered, until the beans are very tender, 2 to 3 hours. Stir the beans occasionally and cover with more water if they become exposed.

Remove the onion, bay leaf, and orange halves (the garlic will likely have melted into the beans). Raise the heat to medium (270°F) and continue cooking until the cooking liquid begins to thicken, about 10 minutes. Season to taste with salt. Top with the cilantro and radishes. Serve over the rice with a lime wedge on the side. Finish with a splash of hot sauce (if using).

1 pound dried black beans, rinsed and picked over

1 yellow onion, sliced in half

1 head garlic, cloves peeled and smashed

1 bay leaf

1 juicing orange, rinsed and sliced in half

Salt

½ cup chopped fresh cilantro

½ cup sliced radishes

4 cups cooked rice

1 lime, cut into 6 wedges

Hot sauce (optional)

Pan-Seared
BRUSSELS SPROUTS

SERVES
4

THESE ARE NOT THE BLAND BRUSSELS SPROUTS you grew up with! The cut side of the sprouts should get nice and browned, with a nutty, buttery flavor enhanced by garlic.

In a large, nonstick, ferrous-bottomed skillet, combine the butter and olive oil over medium-high heat (360°F). When the butter is foamy, reduce the heat to medium-low (180°F). Add the garlic and sprouts, stirring gently until coated. Arrange the sprouts cut-side down and add the water to the skillet. Cover and cook until the sprouts are tender when pierced with a knife, 15 to 20 minutes. Toss with the lemon juice and zest. Season to taste with salt and pepper. Top with the Parmesan just before serving.

1 tablespoon unsalted butter

1 tablespoon olive oil

2 cloves garlic, minced

16 Brussels sprouts, halved lengthwise

2 tablespoons water

Zest and juice from 1 lemon

Salt and freshly ground black pepper

⅓ cup freshly grated Parmesan

GREEN BEANS
with Shaved Parmesan

GET GOURMET FLAVOR IN 5 MINUTES! This side is a perfect accompaniment to the Skillet Chicken with Cherry-Jalapeño Sauce (page 80) or Honey-Glazed Salmon (page 101).

1½ pounds green beans, trimmed

2 tablespoons unsalted butter

2 cloves garlic, minced

½ teaspoon salt

Juice of ½ lemon

Freshly ground black pepper

¼ cup shaved Parmesan

Fill a large ferrous-bottomed pot with lightly salted water and bring to a boil over high heat (450°F). Add the green beans and cook for 3 minutes. Drain the beans and set aside.

In the same pot over medium-high heat (300°F), melt the butter. Add the garlic and salt and cook until fragrant, about 30 seconds to 1 minute. Stir in the green beans and lemon juice. Season to taste with pepper. Cook, tossing until thoroughly combined, for 1 minute longer. Transfer the beans to a serving dish and top with the Parmesan.

Chapter 5
SWEET TREATS

Heavenly
CHOCOLATE SAUCE

2 CUPS

WHAT'S MORE DELICIOUS THAN A SCOOP OF YOUR FAVORITE ICE CREAM? That scoop topped with this decadent chocolate sauce. Because you can maintain a precise low setting with an induction cooktop, this sauce comes together with no double boiler required!

½ cup unsalted butter

¼ cup semisweet chocolate chips

1 cup confectioners' sugar

½ cup unsweetened cocoa powder

1 cup heavy cream

1 teaspoon vanilla extract

Pinch of salt

In a small ferrous-bottomed saucepan, melt the butter and chocolate chips over low heat (150°F), stirring until smooth. Stir in the sugar and cocoa, followed by the cream. Increase the heat to medium (240°F) and cook, stirring occasionally, until the mixture begins to bubble at the sides. Turn off the cooktop and stir in the vanilla and salt.

Let the sauce cool to warm or room temperature before serving. Cover and refrigerate any unused portion for up to 3 days. Reheat gently over low heat.

Peanut Butter–
CHOCOLATE FONDUE

PEANUT BUTTER AND CHOCOLATE . . . that might be all you need to know! But the peanut butter adds even more than yum; it ensures that the fondue reaches a perfect, velvety texture. This dessert makes get-togethers so much more fun and flavorful.

1 cup semisweet chocolate chips

½ cup sugar

½ cup milk

½ cup creamy peanut butter

½ teaspoon vanilla extract

4 large bananas, chopped
into large chunks

1 pint strawberries

6 slices pound cake or angel food cake,
cut into large chunks

In a heavy ferrous-bottomed saucepan over low heat (150°F), combine the chocolate chips, sugar, milk, and peanut butter. Cook, stirring frequently, until smooth. Stir in the vanilla extract. Reduce the heat to the lowest setting to keep warm. Serve with the bananas, strawberries, and cake.

Coconut-Mango
RICE PUDDING

WHY MAKE PUDDING FROM A BOX WHEN YOU CAN COOK up amazing homemade results with just a few simple ingredients? The low, steady heat of an induction cooktop makes cooking puddings exceptionally easy.

In a heavy, ferrous-bottomed 3-quart saucepan over medium heat (270°F), simmer the rice, milk, sugar, and salt, uncovered, stirring frequently, until the rice is tender, about 30 minutes. Stir in the coconut milk and continue to simmer until the liquid is thickened. Stir in the vanilla or coconut extract (if using) and let cool slightly. Serve topped with mango.

1 cup Arborio rice

4 cups milk

½ cup sugar

¼ teaspoon salt

1 can (14 ounces) unsweetened coconut milk

1 teaspoon vanilla or coconut extract (optional)

1 mango, peeled, pitted, and chopped

Creamy BANANA PUDDING

WHILE THIS PUDDING REQUIRES A RELATIVELY SHORT TIME on the cooktop, ideally you should start this recipe early in the day (or the night before) to allow plenty of time for the pudding to cool. The wait is worth it—the flavors only improve with time!

In a 3-quart, ferrous-bottomed saucepan, combine the sugar, flour, and salt. Whisk in the milk and eggs. Cook, stirring frequently, over medium heat (270°F) until the mixture is thick and bubbly, about 7 minutes. Remove from the heat. Stir in the vanilla. Let cool for 15 minutes, stirring occasionally.

In an ungreased 8-inch square baking dish, layer 25 vanilla wafers, half of the banana slices, and half of the pudding. Repeat the layers, ending with a layer of pudding.

Press plastic wrap onto the surface of the pudding. Refrigerate for 4 hours or overnight. Just before serving, remove the wrap; crush the remaining wafers and sprinkle over the top.

¾ cup sugar

¼ cup all-purpose flour

¼ teaspoon salt

3 cups milk

3 large eggs

1½ teaspoons vanilla extract

8 ounces vanilla wafers (about 60 cookies), divided

4 large ripe bananas, cut into ¼-inch slices

Simple
BANANAS FOSTER

SERVES
4

THIS CLASSIC NEW ORLEANS DESSERT IS SO VERY QUICK to make, and it can be just as delicious served without the alcohol often included in recipes. Leftovers, should you be lucky enough to have them, make an excellent topping for French toast or oatmeal.

3 tablespoons unsalted butter

⅓ cup brown sugar

Pinch of ground cinnamon

3 bananas, peeled and sliced lengthwise

1 teaspoon vanilla extract

1 pint vanilla ice cream

Melt the butter in a large, ferrous-bottomed skillet over medium heat (270°F). Add the brown sugar and cinnamon, and cook, stirring, until the sugar dissolves, about 2 minutes. Add the bananas and cook, stirring gently, until the bananas start to soften and brown, about 3 minutes. Turn off the cooktop and stir in the vanilla extract.

Divide the ice cream among 4 dessert bowls. Gently spoon the sauce and bananas over the ice cream and serve immediately.

Poached PEARS

SERVES
4

THESE ELEGANT PEARS ARE A SPLENDID WAY to enjoy a light dessert after a holiday meal. More benefits: they're easy to make on your induction cooktop—and easy to make ahead of time, so you can enjoy the company of your guests.

In a 4-quart ferrous-bottomed saucepan over medium-high heat (300°F), combine the wine, sugar, orange zest and juice, and cinnamon stick. Bring to a boil, reduce the heat to medium-low (180°F), and simmer for 5 minutes.

Gently place the pears in the poaching liquid, cover, and simmer for 15 to 20 minutes, turning every 5 minutes to ensure even color, until the pears are cooked but still firm. Remove the saucepan from the cooktop, uncover, and allow the pears to cool before chilling in the refrigerator for at least 3 hours or up to 24 hours, turning occasionally, if desired.

Before serving, remove the pears from the liquid and allow them to come to room temperature. Meanwhile, transfer the liquid to the saucepan and place over medium-high heat (360°F). Cook until the liquid has reduced and thickened, about 15 minutes. Set the pan on a heatproof surface and cool to room temperature. Serve the pears drizzled with the syrup.

2 cups dry red wine

⅓ cup sugar

Zest and juice of 1 orange

1 cinnamon stick

4 firm, ripe pears, peeled (stem intact)

APPLE CREPES
with Salted Caramel Sauce

THE SECRET TO AMAZING CREPES WITH LESS FUSS: make them early in the day and have them ready and waiting to meet the fruit and sauce for a fabulous dessert. Of course, crepes make a perfectly fine breakfast, too.

CREPES

2 large eggs

½–¾ cup milk

¾ cup all-purpose flour

⅛ teaspoon salt

3 tablespoons unsalted butter

Vegetable oil, for the pan

APPLES AND CARAMEL SAUCE

5 tablespoons unsalted butter

4 large apples (about 2 pounds), peeled, cored, and chopped

⅓ cup granulated sugar

⅓ cup dark brown sugar

½ teaspoon vanilla extract

Pinch of salt

⅓ cup heavy cream

Vanilla ice cream or whipped cream, for serving

TO MAKE THE CREPES: In a blender or food processor fitted with a metal blade, combine the eggs and ½ cup milk. Add the flour and salt and whirl on high speed until smooth, pausing once or twice to scrape down the sides with a rubber spatula. Let the batter rest at room temperature for 30 minutes.

In a small ferrous-bottomed saucepan over medium-low heat (180°F), melt the 3 tablespoons butter and cook until it turns golden brown and has the aroma of toasted nuts, 3 to 5 minutes. Transfer the pan to a heatproof surface, carefully skim off any foam that rises to the top, and let cool slightly. Stir the butter into the batter, which should be the consistency of heavy cream; thin it with more milk, if needed.

Use a brush to coat a ferrous-bottomed crepe pan with a thin layer of oil and place over medium heat (270°F). Add 2 to 3 tablespoons of batter and quickly tilt the pan in all directions to spread the batter evenly over the bottom and a bit up the sides of the pan. Cook until the center of the crepe is set and the bottom is lightly browned, 1 to 2 minutes, depending on the size of the skillet. Flip the crepe and continue cooking until the center is firm and the edges underneath are lightly browned, about 30 seconds. Transfer to a cooling rack. Proceed with the remaining batter, adding more oil to the pan as needed. Once cool, stack the crepes between sheets of wax paper.

TO MAKE THE APPLES AND CARAMEL SAUCE: In a large, heavy ferrous-bottomed skillet over medium heat (270°F), melt the 5 tablespoons butter. Add the apples and sprinkle both sugars over them. Raise the heat to medium-high (330°F). Cook, covered, until the apples begin to soften, about 8 minutes. Uncover and continue to cook, stirring, until the apples are soft, 10 to 12 minutes. (The mixture will be boiling.) Stir in the vanilla and salt. Set aside to cool.

To assemble the crepes, place the crepes flat on a large work surface. Using a slotted spoon, remove the apples from the sauce and divide them among the crepes, spreading them over the surface of each crepe. Fold each crepe to make a half moon and then fold in half again to create a thick triangle.

Bring the remaining sauce back to a boil over medium-high heat (330°F). Add the heavy cream and whisk until the boiling mixture has thickened and darkened again to brown. Serve the crepes with the vanilla ice cream or whipped cream and the sauce drizzled over the top.

White Chocolate CAKE POPS

WHILE AN INDUCTION COOKTOP IS NOT TECHNICALLY an appliance suited to baking, you can still use it to take the cake with impressive desserts! Because it provides such a steady, even temperature, you can use it to melt white chocolate for these fun cake pops. Experiment with different flavor combinations to create your own signature version of this bite-size favorite. Look for lollipop sticks at a craft or cake decorating store.

1 frozen pound cake (10 ounces), thawed and chopped into 1-inch pieces

¼ cup ready-to-spread vanilla frosting

1 package (8 ounces) white chocolate

½ cup sprinkles or candy stars

In the work bowl of a food processor fitted with a metal blade, pulse the cake until it reaches a fine crumb. Add the frosting and pulse again until the mixture comes together. Transfer the mixture to a large bowl and refrigerate, covered, for 30 minutes.

Use a cookie scoop to form the mixture into 18 balls. Arrange on a parchment-lined baking sheet and refrigerate until firm, about 20 minutes.

Meanwhile, in a small, heavy ferrous-bottomed saucepan, warm the white chocolate over medium-low heat (180°F), stirring occasionally, until melted, about 5 minutes. Working in batches, dip the end of a lollipop stick into the chocolate and then insert halfway into a cake pop. Immediately dip the entire cake pop in the coating and then slowly rotate it above the saucepan while the coating drips off. Scatter sprinkles or candy stars on top. Once settled, stand the cake pop up in a heavy-bottomed glass and allow to cool completely before serving.

Fresh
BERRY BUCKLE

**SERVES
6**

THIS LUSCIOUS COBBLER-LIKE DESSERT IS A SNAP to put together and incredibly versatile when seasonal fruits are plentiful. Use your favorite combination of berries, cherries, or peaches for a signature dish. Bonus: By using an induction cooktop in hot weather, you'll keep your kitchen cooler.

In a large ferrous-bottomed nonstick skillet, combine the fruit, ½ cup of the brown sugar, 4 tablespoons of the water, and the salt. Cook over medium heat (270°F) until the fruit softens, about 5 minutes. Meanwhile, in a small bowl, combine the cornstarch and remaining 1 tablespoon water. Add the cornstarch mixture to the fruit and cook, stirring occasionally, until the mixture thickens, about 1 minute longer. Remove the skillet from the cooktop and stir in the vanilla and allspice.

In the work bowl of a food processor fitted with a metal blade, combine the flour, butter, and remaining 2 tablespoons brown sugar. Pulse until the mixture resembles coarse bread crumbs. Transfer the mixture to a mixing bowl and add the buttermilk; stir until combined. Divide the mixture into 6 large spoonfuls and arrange evenly on top of the fruit mixture. Cover and return the skillet to the cooktop. Cook over medium-low heat (210°F) for 10 minutes, until the dumplings are cooked through. Serve warm, topped with the vanilla ice cream (if using).

5 cups mixed fruit, pitted and chopped (if necessary) into uniform pieces

½ cup plus 2 tablespoons packed brown sugar, divided

5 tablespoons cold water, divided

⅛ teaspoon salt

1 tablespoon cornstarch

1 teaspoon vanilla extract

¼ teaspoon ground allspice

½ cup all-purpose flour

2 tablespoons cold, unsalted butter

¼ cup buttermilk

Vanilla ice cream, for serving (optional)

Blueberry
CREAM PIE

BLUEBERRIES AND FRESH CREAM ARE A WINNING combination. Best of all, you can use either fresh or frozen berries, which means it's easy to put together any time of year. The whipped cream gets a boost of flavor from the lemon zest, though you could add the zest to the blueberries instead.

¾ cup granulated sugar

3 tablespoons cornstarch

¼ teaspoon salt

⅔ cup water

3 cups (1½ pints) fresh or frozen blueberries, divided

2 tablespoons unsalted butter

Juice and zest from ½ lemon

1 cup heavy cream

2 tablespoons confectioners' sugar

½ teaspoon vanilla extract

1 (9-inch) prebaked pie crust

In a medium, ferrous-bottomed pot over medium heat (270°F), combine the granulated sugar, cornstarch, salt, water, and 1 cup of the blueberries. Cook, stirring constantly, until the mixture comes to a boil and thickens, about 10 minutes. Turn off the heat. Add the butter and lemon juice. When the mixture is cooled to room temperature, stir in the remaining 2 cups blueberries. Transfer the mixture to a glass bowl and refrigerate, covered, for at least an hour or up to 6 hours.

Using a stand mixture with a wire whisk attachment, whip the cream until thick. Add the confectioners' sugar, vanilla, and lemon zest. Whip again until thoroughly combined. Cover the bottom of the pie crust with half of the whipped cream, then pour the blueberry filling on top. Cover with plastic wrap and chill for 2 hours. Cover and refrigerate the remaining whipped cream. Top the pie with the reserved whipped cream just before serving.

Cherry- CHEESE PIE

THIS CHOCOLATE-CRUSTED PIE WILL DRAW RAVE REVIEWS. Of course, if you prefer a regular graham cracker crumb, that will work nicely, too. Whichever way you go, take your time spreading the cheese mixture so that it is evenly applied.

Drain the cherries, reserving the juice. Set both aside.

In a medium, ferrous-bottomed saucepan, combine ⅔ cup of the sugar, cornstarch, and salt. Add 1 cup of the reserved juice and cook over medium heat (270°F), stirring constantly, until the mixture comes to a boil. Cook an additional 2 minutes, add the cherries, and continue cooking for another 2 minutes. Turn off the heat and add the butter and lemon juice. Let the mixture cool to room temperature.

Using a mixer fitted with a paddle attachment, beat the cream cheese, remaining ⅓ cup sugar, and vanilla until fluffy. Spread the cheese mixture evenly over the bottom of the pie crust. Top with the cherry filling. Cover loosely with plastic wrap and refrigerate at least 3 hours or up to 8 hours before serving.

2 cans (16 ounces) pitted dark sweet cherries

1 cup sugar, divided

3 tablespoons cornstarch

⅛ teaspoon salt

1 tablespoon butter

2 tablespoons fresh lemon juice

1 package (3 ounces) cream cheese, softened

1 teaspoon vanilla extract

1 (9-inch) prepared chocolate crumb pie crust

Chocolate
CREAM PIE

HERE'S A DECADENT VERSION OF AN AMERICAN CLASSIC. A rich layer of chocolate custard sits between a flaky pie crust and soft clouds of whipped cream. Be sure to start this pie well ahead of when you plan to serve it so that it has time to set up properly.

2 ounces (about ⅓ cup) semisweet chocolate chips

2 ounces baking chocolate, chopped

1 cup plus 2 tablespoons sugar, divided

¼ cup all-purpose flour

1 tablespoon cornstarch

¼ teaspoon salt

4 large egg yolks

3 cups milk

2 tablespoons unsalted butter

1½ teaspoons vanilla extract

1 (9-inch) prebaked pie crust

1 cup heavy cream

Cocoa powder or chocolate sprinkles, for garnish

In a small, heavy ferrous-bottomed saucepan, melt both chocolates over low heat (150°F), stirring occasionally, until smooth. Place the pan on a heatproof surface.

In a medium, ferrous-bottomed saucepan, whisk together 1 cup of the sugar, flour, cornstarch, salt, and egg yolks until thoroughly combined. Whisk in the milk and bring the mixture to a boil over medium-high heat (300°F), whisking frequently. When the mixture boils, reduce the heat to medium-low (180°F) and simmer until thick, about 1 minute longer.

Force the custard through a fine-mesh sieve into a medium bowl and then whisk in the melted chocolate, butter, and vanilla until smooth. Transfer the filling to the pie crust and then refrigerate, covered, for at least 6 hours or overnight.

Before serving, whip the cream until soft peaks form. Add the remaining 2 tablespoons sugar and continue whipping until stiff peaks form. Spoon the whipped cream on top of the pie and finish with a dusting of cocoa powder or chocolate sprinkles. Serve immediately.

Fruit FRITTERS

YOUR INDUCTION COOKTOP IS A GREAT TOOL FOR FRYING because it is well designed to hold a pan at a steady temperature. You can use just about any fresh seasonal fruit in this easy-to-make batter. Serve with ice cream if you like.

In a ferrous-bottomed Dutch oven over medium-high heat (360°F), heat 3 inches of oil to 360°F, adjusting the settings as necessary to maintain a steady temperature.

While the oil is warming, in a medium bowl, sift together the flour, granulated sugar, baking powder, and salt. Add the egg yolks and milk and stir until thoroughly combined. In a large bowl, use a mixer to whip the egg whites until stiff peaks form. Fold the egg whites into the batter mixture.

When the oil is hot, dip a few pieces of fruit into the batter and let any excess drip off. Use tongs to carefully slide the fruit into the hot oil and fry, turning once, until golden brown and puffed, 3 to 4 minutes. Drain on paper towels and sprinkle with the confectioners' sugar before serving.

Vegetable oil, for frying

1 cup all-purpose flour

1 tablespoon granulated sugar

1 teaspoon baking powder

½ teaspoon salt

2 large eggs, separated

½ cup milk

4 cups bite-size pieces of fruit, such as apple, banana, strawberries, or nectarines

Confectioners' sugar, for garnish

Best
BEIGNETS

IF YOU'VE EVER BEEN TO NEW ORLEANS, you know that beignets are the bomb. For an authentic Big Easy experience, enjoy these with a strong cup of chicory coffee. If you have a stand mixer with a dough hook, let it help you with this recipe.

2¼ teaspoons (one ¼-ounce package) active dry yeast

1½ cups warm water

½ cup granulated sugar

1 teaspoon salt

2 eggs, lightly beaten

1 cup evaporated milk

7 cups all-purpose flour, divided

¼ cup shortening

Vegetable oil, for frying

Sifted confectioners' sugar

In a large bowl, sprinkle the yeast over the warm water. Stir to dissolve and let stand until foamy, about 5 minutes.

Add the granulated sugar, salt, eggs, and evaporated milk and beat until thoroughly combined. Add 4 cups of the flour, in 2 batches if necessary, and beat until smooth. Beat in the shortening, then gradually mix in the remaining 3 cups flour. Cover with plastic wrap and refrigerate for at least 4 hours or overnight.

On a lightly floured work surface, roll out the dough to a thickness of ¼ inch. Cut into 2½ x 3-inch rectangles and set aside.

In a ferrous-bottomed Dutch oven over medium-high heat (360°F), heat 3 inches of oil to 360°F, adjusting the settings as necessary to maintain a steady temperature. When the oil is hot, work in small batches of 3 or 4 to carefully slide the beignets into the hot oil and fry, turning once, until golden brown and puffed, 2 to 3 minutes. Drain on paper towels and sprinkle with confectioners' sugar before serving.

Old-Fashioned
CIDER DOUGHNUTS

MAKES
20

A NEW ENGLAND HARVEST-TIME FAVORITE, these delicious cake doughnuts are sure to bring smiles any time of year. Your induction cooktop helps you get just the right temperature for easy frying. Little hands can help with the shaping and glazing.

TO MAKE THE GLAZE: In a small bowl, combine the ¼ cup cider and confectioners' sugar. Set aside.

TO MAKE THE DOUGHNUTS: In a small ferrous-bottomed saucepan over medium-high heat (300°F), boil the 1 cup cider until it is reduced to ¼ cup, 8 to 10 minutes. Set aside to cool.

In a large bowl, combine the flour, baking powder, baking soda, allspice, salt, and nutmeg. Mix until thoroughly combined. Set aside.

In another large bowl, combine the shortening and granulated sugar. Beat with a mixer until smooth. Add the eggs, buttermilk, and reduced cider, beating after each addition until thoroughly combined. Add the flour mixture and mix until thoroughly combined. Transfer the dough to a lightly floured work surface and pat to a ½ inch thickness. Use a 2½-inch doughnut cutter to cut the doughnuts, reshaping the dough as necessary until all the doughnuts are formed. Let rest for 5 minutes before frying.

In a ferrous-bottomed Dutch oven over medium-high heat (360°F), heat 3 inches of oil to 360°F, adjusting the settings as necessary to maintain a steady temperature. When the oil is hot, work in small batches of 3 or 4 to carefully slide the doughnuts into the hot oil and fry, turning once, until golden brown, 2 to 3 minutes. Drain on paper towels. When the doughnuts are cool enough to handle, dip them in the cider glaze before serving.

GLAZE

¼ cup apple cider

2 cups confectioners' sugar

DOUGHNUTS

1 cup apple cider

3½ cups all-purpose flour

2 teaspoons baking powder

1 teaspoon baking soda

½ teaspoon ground allspice

½ teaspoon salt

¼ teaspoon ground nutmeg

¼ cup shortening

1 cup granulated sugar

2 large eggs

½ cup buttermilk

Vegetable oil, for frying

Candied
ORANGE SLICES

YOU CAN USE THESE DELICATE ORANGE SLICES to garnish cakes, top ice cream, or add an interesting accent to salads. There really is no limit to their potential! When you're finished, be sure to refrigerate the leftover syrup for cocktails.

3 oranges

2 cups sugar

2 tablespoons fresh orange juice

2 cups water

Fill a large bowl with ice water and set aside. Slice the oranges into ⅛-inch rounds, discarding the seeds and end pieces. You should get 8 slices per orange.

Fill a medium, ferrous-bottomed pot with water and bring to a boil over high heat (450°F). Add the orange slices and boil for 1 minute. Drain the pot and transfer the orange slices to the bowl of ice water to cool. Drain thoroughly.

In a large, ferrous-bottomed saucepan over medium-high heat (360°F), combine the sugar, orange juice, and water. Bring the mixture to a boil and cook until the sugar dissolves. Reduce the heat to medium-low (180°F), add the orange slices, and simmer, turning occasionally, until the orange rinds are translucent, about 1 hour. Transfer the orange slices to a cooling rack and let cool completely overnight. Refrigerate in an airtight container until ready to use. Let the syrup cool completely before straining and refrigerating for another use.

Candied GINGER

1½ CUPS

IF YOU'VE EVER BOUGHT CANDIED GINGER for a recipe, you know it's expensive stuff. But you can make your own for a fraction of the cost and enjoy an added by-product—ginger syrup! Pour it over waffles or ice cream, add a spoonful to your tea, or stir it into a glass of club soda for a homemade version of ginger ale.

2 large hands fresh ginger, peeled

3½ cups sugar, divided

3 cups water

Slice the ginger into ⅛-inch thick pieces.

In a large, ferrous-bottomed saucepan over medium-high heat (360°F), combine 3 cups of the sugar and the water. Bring the mixture to a boil and cook until the sugar dissolves. Reduce the heat to medium-low (180°F), add the ginger, and simmer, stirring occasionally, until the ginger is tender, about 45 minutes. Transfer the ginger pieces to a cooling rack and let cool completely, about 30 minutes. Raise the heat to medium (270°F) and boil the remaining syrup until it is the consistency of honey. Let cool completely before straining and refrigerating the syrup for another use.

When the ginger pieces are cool enough to handle, toss them in the remaining ½ cup sugar and scatter evenly over a piece of wax paper to continue drying, preferably overnight. Store the ginger pieces in an airtight container for up to 2 weeks.

Homemade CARAMELS

USING AN INDUCTION COOKTOP MAKES IT EASIER to produce amazing caramels, but you'll still need to use a candy thermometer to make sure you achieve the correct temperatures. Caramels are an unforgiving candy, with caramel sauce or a brittle toffee being the results of too little or too long on the cooktop.

Line a 9 x 5-inch loaf pan with aluminum foil and brush lightly with vegetable oil. Set aside.

In a small ferrous-bottomed pot over medium heat (270°F), warm the cream, vanilla, salt, and 2 tablespoons of the butter, stirring occasionally, until the butter is melted. Set aside.

In a medium (2-quart) ferrous-bottomed pot over medium–high heat (330°F), combine the sugar and corn syrup. Cook, stirring occasionally, until the sugar dissolves (use a wet pastry brush to wash away any sugar that clings to the side of the pot). Cook without stirring until a candy thermometer reads 310°F.

Transfer the pot to a heatproof surface and slowly pour the cream mixture into the syrup (it will bubble aggressively, so be careful and work slowly). Stir until smooth. Place the pot back on the cooktop and cook until the thermometer reads 260°F. Turn off the cooktop and stir in the remaining 2 tablespoons butter. When the mixture is smooth, transfer it to the prepared loaf pan. Let cool completely, preferably overnight.

Remove the caramel from the pan by lifting the foil. Peel the foil from the caramel and cut into 35 pieces. Wrap each caramel individually with wax paper.

¾ cup heavy cream

1 teaspoon vanilla extract

¾ teaspoon salt, preferably kosher

4 tablespoons unsalted butter, divided

1 cup sugar

½ cup vanilla-flavored corn syrup

Everyone's Favorite
PEANUT BRITTLE

1½ POUNDS

THIS CANDY IS PERFECT FOR GIFT GIVING! For a change of pace, try substituting cashews or almonds in place of the peanuts. And for a little extra kick, add a pinch of cayenne pepper to the pot along with the butter and baking soda.

2 cups sugar

1 cup corn syrup

1 cup water

½ teaspoon salt

2 cups raw peanuts

2 tablespoons unsalted butter

2 teaspoons baking soda

Line 2 rimmed baking sheets with parchment paper. Set aside.

In a large ferrous-bottomed saucepan over medium heat (270°F), combine the sugar, corn syrup, water, and salt. Cook, stirring occasionally, until the sugar dissolves (use a wet pastry brush to wash away any sugar that clings to the side of the pot). Cook without stirring until a candy thermometer reads 250°F.

Add the peanuts and continue cooking, stirring frequently, until the thermometer reads 300°F. Transfer the pot to a heatproof surface. Add the butter and baking soda. Stir vigorously until the butter is melted. Pour the mixture onto the prepared baking sheets, spreading with a silicone spatula until it is in an even layer. When completely cooled, break into pieces and store in an airtight container until you're ready to serve.

INDEX